MW01626823

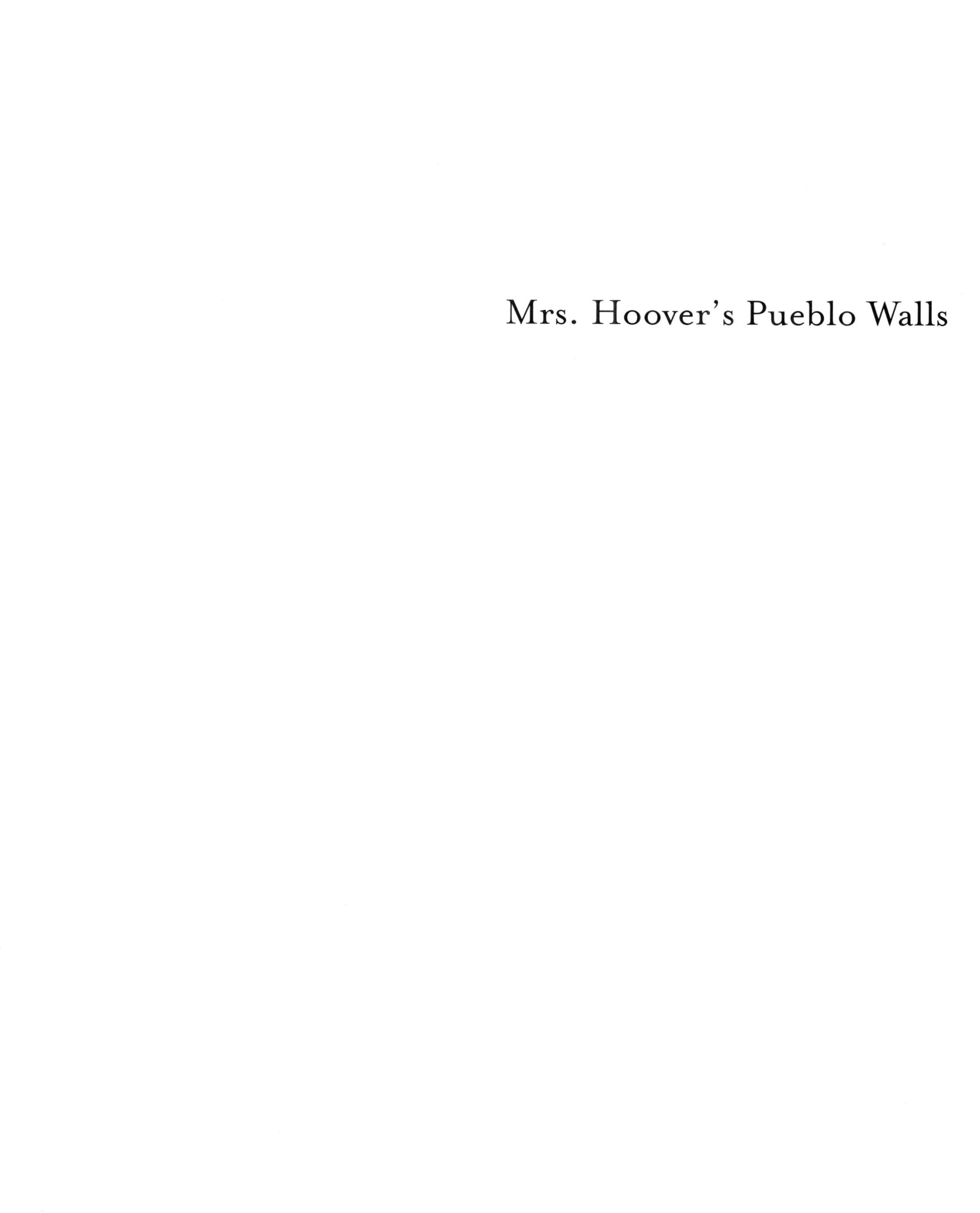

Mrs. Hoover's Pueblo Walls

Hoover House from the northeast, 1975. Photograph by Jack Boucher. (Courtesy Stanford University Archives)

Mrs. Hoover's Pueblo Walls

THE PRIMITIVE AND THE MODERN IN THE LOU HENRY HOOVER HOUSE

Paul V. Turner

STANFORD UNIVERSITY PRESS
STANFORD, CALIFORNIA 2004

Stanford University Press
Stanford, California

Printed in the United States of America on acid-free, archival-quality paper

Library of Congress Cataloging-in-Publication Data

Turner, Paul Venable.
Mrs. Hoover's pueblo walls : the primitive and the modern in the Lou Henry Hoover House / Paul V. Turner.
p. cm.
Includes bibliographical references and index.
ISBN 0-8047-3941-2 (cloth : alk. paper)
1. Lou Henry Hoover House (Stanford, Calif.) 2. Hoover, Lou Henry, 1874–1944—Homes and haunts—California—Stanford. 3. Hoover, Herbert, 1874–1964—Homes and haunts—California—Stanford. 4. Architecture, Domestic—California—Stanford. 5. Architecture—California—Stanford—20th century. 6. College presidents—Dwellings—California—Stanford. 7. Stanford (Calif.)—Buildings, structures, etc. I. Title.
NA7238.S8T87 2004
728.8'09794'73—dc22 2004006723

Original Printing 2004

Last figure below indicates year of this printing:
13 12 11 10 09 08 07 06 05 04

Designed by Janet Wood
Typeset by Classic Typography
in 11/14 Adobe Garamond

At the door I spoke of the beauty of her house [the Hoovers' house in Washington DC, before Herbert's election as president] and said that the next time I saw her she might be in a still more beautiful one. Naturally I was thinking of the White House.

"Yes," she replied with a gay laugh, "you *must* come to see us in California!"

—From an article reporting an interview with Lou Henry Hoover during the presidential campaign of 1928 ("Electing a President's Wife," *Woman's Home Companion*, April 1928, p. 64)

Why wouldn't it be a good idea (for me!) for you to take on the job of "official hostess" on the hill for the next month? A few people will be staying with us, and I have no idea whether it will be two or three, or sixteen with a cot in every hall! Bert does in such matters what appeals to him at the moment. . . . So I have no idea what the demands will be for sleeping and feeding people inside the pueblo walls.

—Letter from Lou Henry Hoover to friend Susan Dyer, July 13, 1928 (Hoover Institution Archives)

CONTENTS

ILLUSTRATIONS

last year, the Leland Stanford Junior University Marching Band did precisely that, surprising her with a serenade from up above. The image of the lively group on the roof brought to mind the historic photo of the house (Fig. 36) on the evening of Herbert Hoover's election in November 1928, when a crowd of people occupied the upper terraces.

We think Mrs. Hoover would delight in the knowledge that the home she took great care in planning has met the varied needs of its occupants for so many years, and we hope she would be pleased to see the delight on the faces of the thousands of visitors who come to the house each year. Of course, as with most old homes, there have been some changes within, but the essentials of the original house remain intact. In speaking to us about the Lou Henry Hoover House, former presidents, first ladies, their children, as well as university students have all expressed a fondness for the house and nostalgia about the time they spent here. When the time comes, we are sure that we too will have enjoyed the privilege of living in Hoover House and will remember it fondly.

John and Andrea Hennessy

PREFACE

Stanford University has much fine architecture—such as the Quad, designed in the 1880s by Frederick Law Olmsted and Charles Coolidge, and the Hanna House, Frank Lloyd Wright's innovative residence constructed in 1937. But the most intriguing Stanford building is probably the Hoover House, built by Herbert and Lou Henry Hoover in 1919–20 and now the official residence of the university president. It is intriguing mainly for two reasons: the identity of its architect has been unclear, and there has been much uncertainty about its architectural sources and style.

As an architectural historian, I have frequently been asked about the house, especially, "What kind of architecture is it?" or "What style is it?" Over the years, I made occasional forays into the archives of the Stanford library, attempting to identify the building's architect and the inspiration for its design. The more I delved into the records, the more interesting the story became. In 1999 I gave a lecture on the house for the Stanford Historical Society; following the talk, I was encouraged to develop my findings and interpretations for publication.

This book focuses on selected aspects of the story of the Hoover House, in particular those most relevant to the questions about its architect and the sources of its design. Other parts of the story are not examined, or are touched on only lightly, such as the building's structural properties, its interior decor, and its use by Stanford presidents and their families after the house was given to the university. In essence, this work is my attempt to answer the inquiries most frequently made about the house.

I thank the following people for their help in this project: Margaret J. Kimball, Stanford University Archivist, and Christy Smith, Library Specialist; Elena S. Danielson, director of the Hoover Library and Archives, Hoover Institution, and Heather Wagner, Archival Specialist; the staff of the Herbert Hoover Presidential Library, West Branch, Iowa; George H. Nash and Susan E. Kennedy, Hoover scholars; Richard Joncas, coauthor of *Stanford University, The Campus Guide*, who shared with me his research on the Hoover House; Herbert Hoover III and

Margaret Ann Hoover Brigham, Hoover family members; Norris Pope, editor at the Stanford University Press; and Gerhard Casper, former president of Stanford University, who encouraged this work in its early stages.

I also acknowledge my debt to Birge Clark, who was involved in the design of the Hoover House and oversaw its construction at the beginning of his architectural career. Shortly after arriving at Stanford in 1971, I had the pleasure of getting to know Clark, who was then in his eighties and still practicing architecture. During our conversations, he did not tell me much about the Hoover House, but having met him increased my interest in the building once I became familiar with it, and his extensive writings and interviews about it have proven crucial to my study.

FIGURE 2 Hoover House from the north, 1920s. (Courtesy Hoover Institution Archives)

ter from the exterior, with decor and furnishings drawn mainly from European traditions. But it is the building's exterior that has aroused the most interest, and despite its eclectic details the exterior is not a pastiche. Overall, it has a distinctive character created by several dominant traits: massive and cubic forms, plain surfaces, and flat roofs, which are probably the most unusual feature of the house for its time. It is this stark, cubic character that makes the Hoover House especially noteworthy and has caused observers to wonder about its style and sources.

The Hoovers themselves and the architects who executed the house did occasionally address this question, but their remarks were often ambiguous or even contradictory. In his memoirs, Herbert called the building "a Hopi house," and Lou affectionately referred to her "pueblo walls."[5] But in her only known discussion of the question, Lou wrote that she and her husband were not "trying to make a pueblo period house, as the design was determined mainly by practical needs"—although she implied that she was inspired by "primitive" architecture from many parts of the world. The building's architect of record, Arthur Bridgman Clark, named Mediterranean and Southwest American architecture as prototypes. Clark's son Birge Clark, who also worked on the project, spoke of

FIGURE 3 Hoover House, aerial view from the northeast, before 1935. (Courtesy Stanford University Archives)

"Algerian" sources, but in later years he denied stylistic influences, writing, "It has frequently been called Algerian or Pueblo Indian; this is purely coincidental."[5]

Another interpretation of the house is that it was simply unconventional or iconoclastic. The elder Clark commented, "The individuality of the owner [is] evidenced everywhere by the lack of conventionality and disregard of tradition or the accepted way of doing things."[6] And in an interview many years later, the younger Clark wrote, "Neither of them [the Hoovers] wanted the house to be . . . any historical style. They just wanted it to be a house."[7]

This study will argue that most of these views have some validity, as the Hoover House incorporates many sources and motives. One facet of the Hoovers' temperament, perhaps reflecting their scientific and engineering backgrounds, tended toward an architectural ideal of functionalism and practicality. Especially in the case of Mrs. Hoover, however, there was also a strong aesthetic concern, as shown by the accounts of her study of visual effects during the design of the house and remarks such as "I wanted to make it just as simple in line and surface as could be done."[8]

The interplay of diverse ideals and motives—functionalist, aesthetic, and cultural or historical—produced a unique structure that expressed the complex personalities of its builders. At the same time, this very personal creation bears similarities to the dominant form of modern architecture that was just beginning to emerge in Europe and would later be named the "International Style." There are fundamental differences between the Hoover House and International-Style

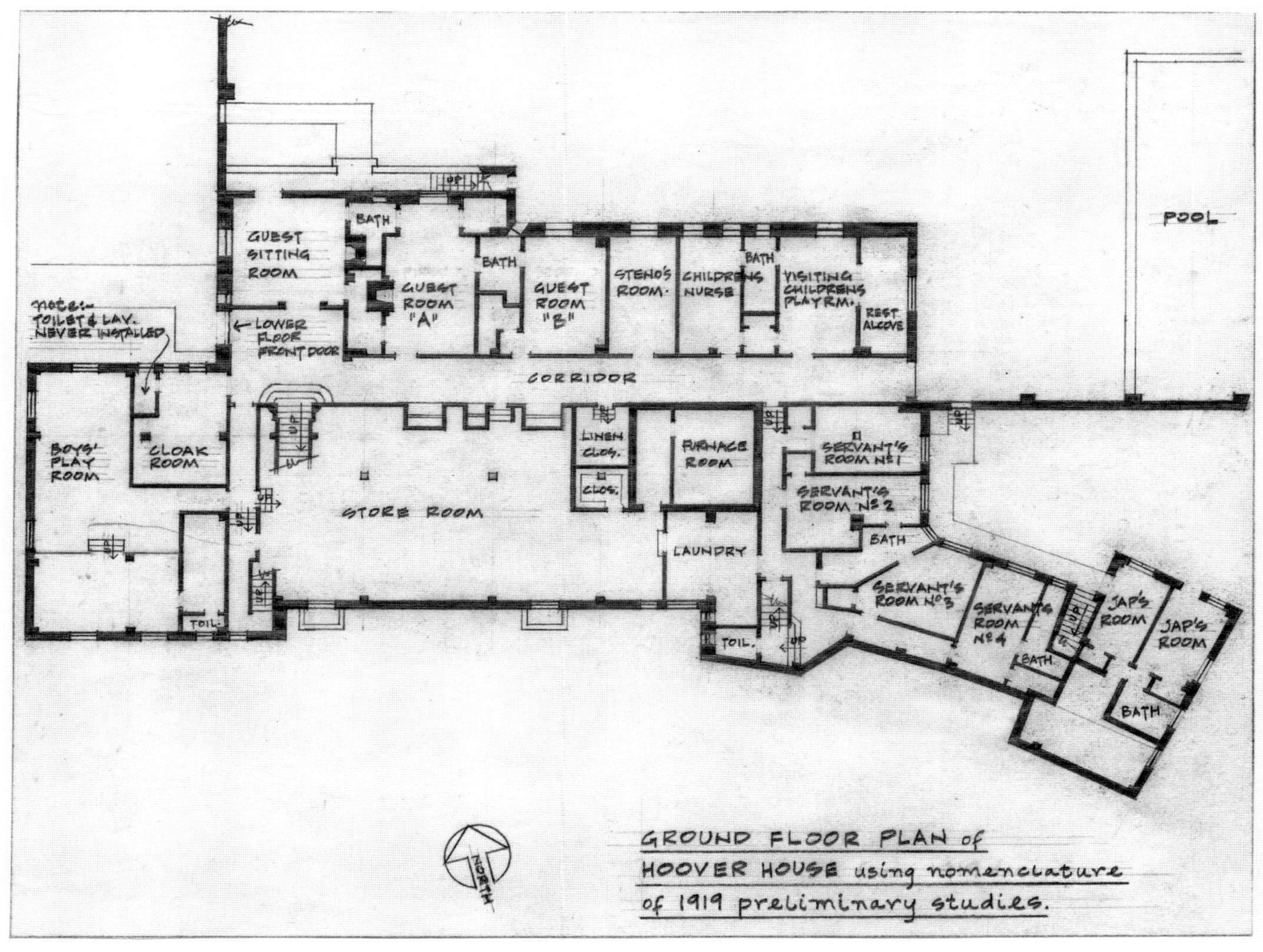

FIGURE 4 Hoover House, plan of ground floor, redrawn in 1960s from 1919 drawings. (Courtesy Stanford University Archives)

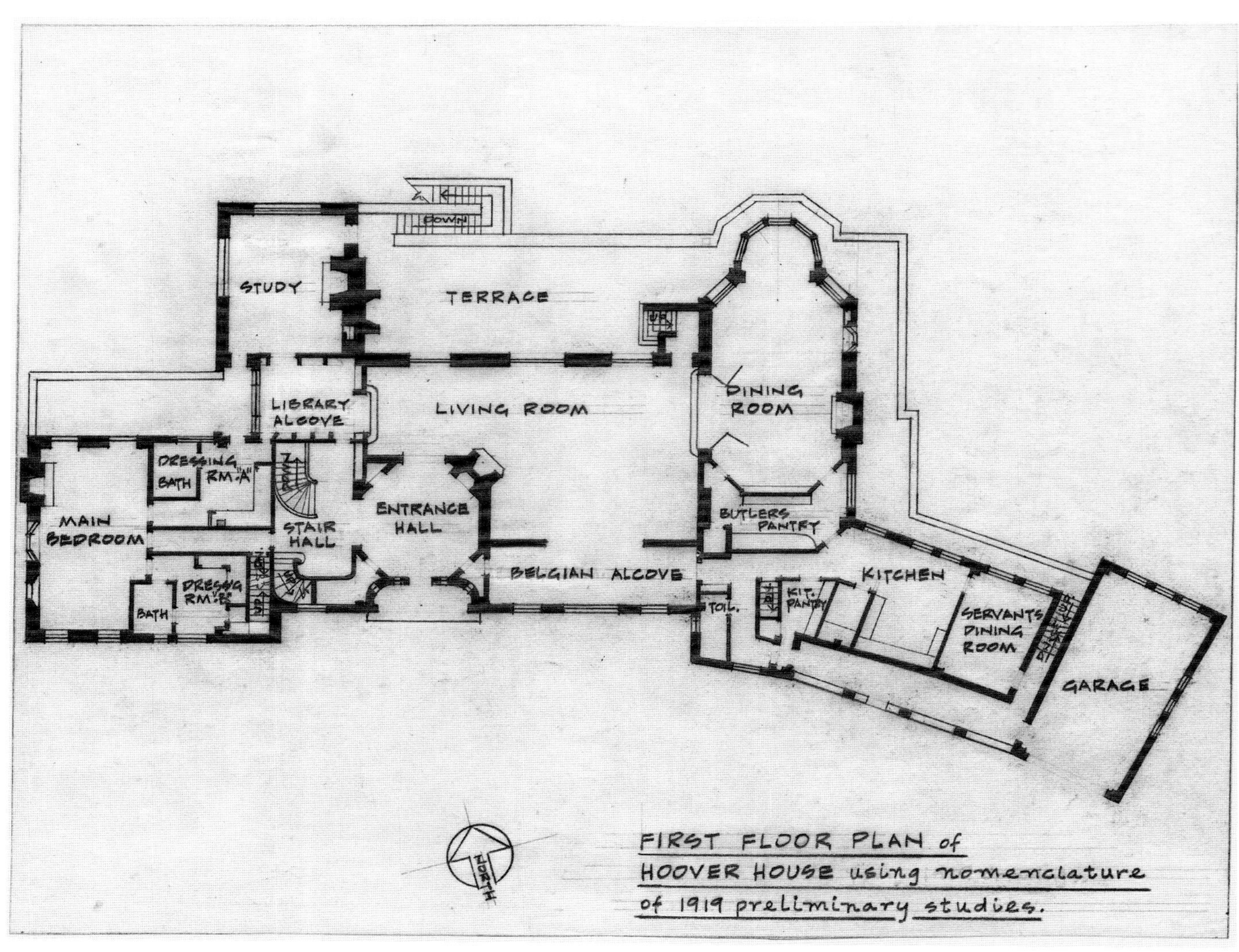

FIGURE 5 Hoover House, plan of first floor. Note: the north arrow on these plans is not precise; the terrace on this level faces northeast. (Courtesy Stanford University Archives)

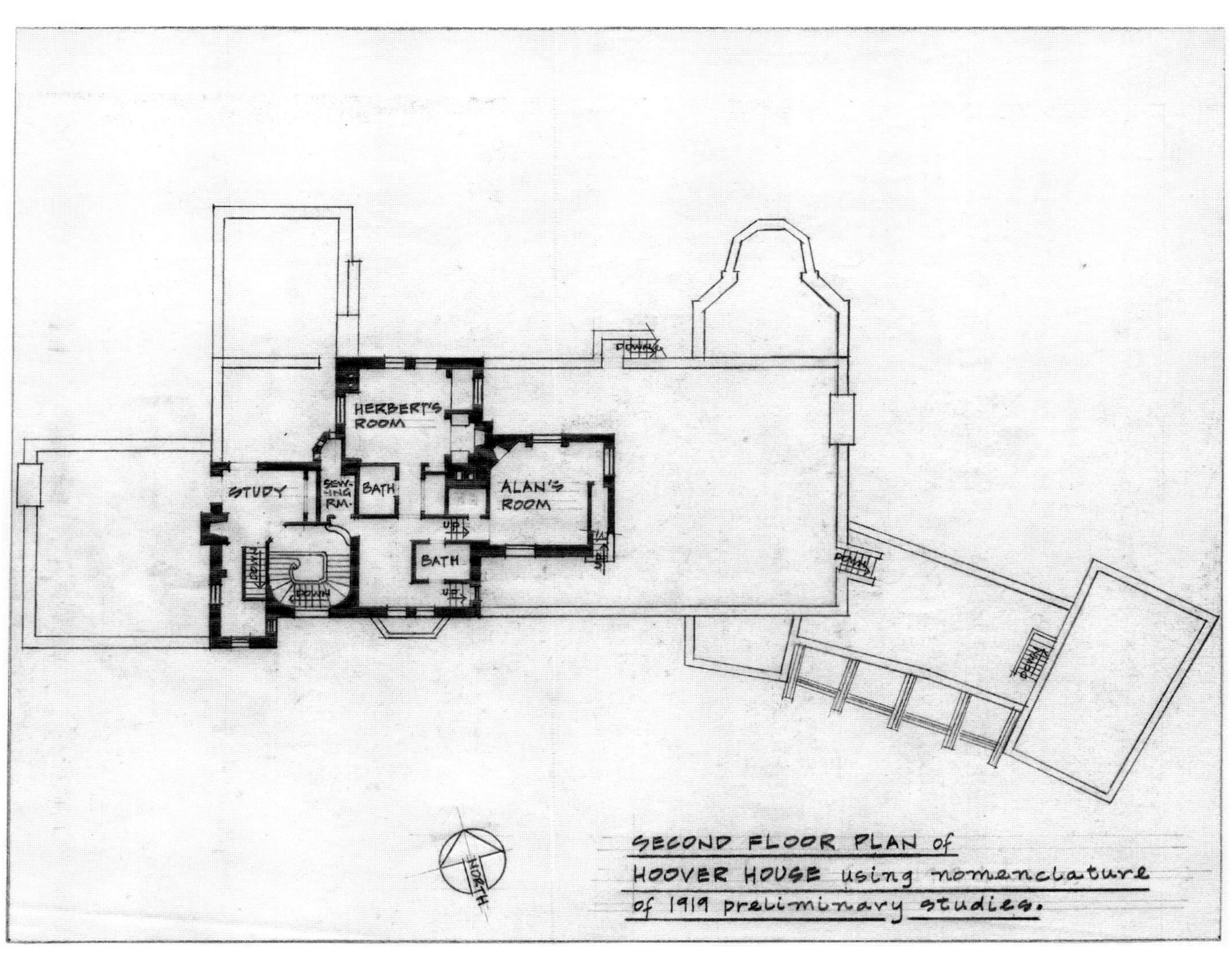

FIGURE 6 Hoover House, plan of second floor. (Courtesy Stanford University Archives)

FIGURE 7 Hoover House from the west, shortly after construction. (Courtesy Hoover Institution Archives)

buildings, but the traits common to them—especially stark, cubic forms, arranged asymmetrically—are strong enough that at first glance the Hoover House is sometimes mistaken for an International-Style building of the 1920s or 1930s. The house also has similarities to the work of Irving Gill in Southern California of the 1910s; but neither can this account fully for the character of the Hoover House. The various explanations that have been proposed for the design of the building will be examined in Chapter 3.

It appears that the Hoovers were influenced by several cultural trends that were developing in the early years of the twentieth century, which later coalesced into high-style "modern" architecture, but which occasionally found expression also in the work of nonprofessionals or amateurs. Among these trends were an attraction to pure, undecorated geometric forms; an adherence to functionalism, at least in principle (the resulting architecture was not necessarily as functional as it looked); a passion for healthy living and outdoor activity; and a fascination with the "primitive" forms of non-European cultures.

The Hoover House illustrates a little-studied phenomenon in early twentieth-century architecture, in which buildings created by amateurs—or by professionals

FIGURE 8 Hoover House from the west, 2003. (Norris Pope)

not associated with the modernist movement—possessed traits that in progressive circles would develop into International-Style modernism. Not surprisingly, these outsider creations often incorporated idiosyncratic features alien to the purer versions of modernism: inconsistent forms, references to traditional styles, or constructional techniques not fully modern. As a result, this architecture tended to be ambiguous in nature, or only quasi modern, at least in the eyes of later observers once the International Style had been codified and accepted as the standard of modernism.

Examples of this quasi-modern architecture are worth examining, both because of the inherent quality they may have and because of the role they played in the cultural scene of their time, serving as a kind of transition to modernism, or as a stimulus to the general public to consider new principles of design. The Hoover House provides a good case study of this phenomenon, because of its early date and because the fame of its owners resulted in extensive publicity and commentary about it.

To speak of the Hoover House as a nonprofessional or amateur work requires explanation, since professional architects were involved in its creation. The question of who, in fact, designed the building has been discussed ever since its construction. Three professionals participated in the project: Arthur B. Clark, a professor

FIGURE 9 Hoover House, part of garden side of house, with Herbert Hoover's office at right. (Norris Pope)

FIGURE 10 (*opposite*) Hoover House, page of photographs in *San Francisco Chronicle*, July 1, 1928. (Courtesy Hoover Institution Archives and *San Francisco Chronicle*)

HOOVER'S HOME *at Stanford*

623 MIRADA DRIVE
The grey stucco house on San Juan Hill above Stanford University, where the Republican presidential nominee maintains his California home.

THE DRAWING ROOM
(Right) Spacious rooms with low ceiling are characteristic of the house, which also reflects the Quaker-Dutch heritage of Herbert Hoover.

AN UPPER HALLWAY
Here is revealed the simplicity that is the keynote of the house.

TYPICALLY CALIFORNIAN
The Hoover home is in the so-called Mission-Pueblo style of architecture. This is the front or west side of the house, directly upon the drive.

THE UPPER TERRACE
From this quiet spot, ideal for quiet meditation, one looks out over the broad campus of Stanford University.

THE DINING ROOM
The formal appearance of this room reminds one of the severity of the cabinet room at the White House.

VIEW FROM THE GARDEN
Trees, shrubs, vines and flowers run riot about the house and grounds.

HISTORY WILL BE MADE HERE
Study where "H. H." will confer with the party leaders. The library is seen through the doorway.

THE SWIMMING POOL
The solid comfort and quiet beauty of the Hoover home, which was built as a present for Mrs. Hoover, are here depicted.

—*Photos by Wide World*

of art and design at Stanford, whose name appears as the architect on the working drawings for the house; his son Birge M. Clark, a young architect who entered the scene in the middle of the project and contributed to the subsequent work; and a draftsman named Charles T. Davis. But it was acknowledged, from the beginning, that Lou Henry Hoover played the major role in the design. Arthur Clark told her frankly, in a letter early in the design process, "My idea of this architectural project is that . . . you are the architect-in-chief."[9] Birge Clark later recalled that his father understood from the start that Mrs. Hoover was to "act as the architect," and that Charles Davis did "the major part of the work" but was "quite in awe of Mrs. Hoover."[10] Birge's description of a typical visit by Mrs. Hoover to the drafting table will be quoted later.

It is not uncommon for architects to compliment their clients by acknowledging their contributions to a design. Normally this means simply that the client had ideas about the overall layout of the house, its general appearance, or specific details, while it was the architect who integrated all the elements and gave the design a unified character or style. In the case of the Hoover House, however, the evidence shows that Lou Henry Hoover played a much more important role than this, and that the stylistic nature of the house was created mainly by her. This is shown by the story of the design process and is supported also by the fact that the house is different from the other buildings designed by Arthur Clark and by Birge Clark.

Although Mrs. Hoover had no architectural training, she had great interest in buildings and was involved in several other architectural projects during her life. She later stated, in fact, that she wished she could have been a professional architect. There can be no doubt that Lou was the major creative force in the design of the house.

It also appears that Herbert played more of a role than previously thought. He was in Washington and elsewhere, serving in the Wilson administration, during most of the design process, and his few recorded remarks about the house imply that he had only minimal interest in its design. But it will be argued here that he made more of a contribution than he acknowledged.

The story of the Hoover House is of interest for the light it sheds on one type of early modern architecture in America. It also helps us understand the characters of Herbert and Lou Henry Hoover.

Chapter One LOU HENRY AND HERBERT HOOVER

The Hoover House in many ways embodies the personalities, ideals, and experiences of Lou Henry and Herbert Hoover (Figs. 11–12). To appreciate the house requires some understanding of them, especially of Lou, the principal designer of the building.

The house's location itself, at Stanford University, was significant to the Hoovers. They had met and courted as undergraduates at Stanford, both majoring in geology—Herbert in the class of 1895 (he had entered as a freshman in the first class when Stanford opened in 1891) and Lou Henry in the class of 1898. The day after they married, in 1899, they embarked for China, and for the next decade and a half they continually moved from one part of the world to another, as Herbert pursued his meteoric career as a mining engineer and businessman. They maintained a house in London, where Herbert's firm was headquartered, but for years they dreamed of creating a home in America, and Stanford was the place fondest to them. Even the specific site of the house, on San Juan Hill, was reportedly chosen for sentimental reasons. Birge Clark, who worked with Lou on the design of the building, later recalled that this site "had been decided upon because as students both the Hoovers had enjoyed walking up onto this hill."[1] Herbert himself said that his wife "had long dreamed of building a house upon a near-by campus hill where the glorious views of the mountains and bay came into sight."[2]

In 1908 the Hoovers began living part-time in Palo Alto and on the Stanford campus, in a succession of rented and purchased houses. Herbert became involved in the governance of the university, as a member of Stanford's board of trustees starting in 1912 and as a benefactor of the institution. He was the main force, for example, behind the creation of the student union and was the anonymous donor of much of the funding for construction of its first buildings, the Men's Clubhouse and Women's Clubhouse (the wings of the complex now called the Old Union), with Lou raising funds specifically for the Women's Clubhouse.[3] Creating their permanent home at Stanford was an affirmation of their strong ties to this place. For Lou, moreover, the design of the house was intended

FIGURE 11 Lou Henry Hoover in London, 1914. (Courtesy Hoover Institution Archives)

to harmonize with the architecture of the university and, more generally, with the character of California and the American West.

The Hoovers epitomized a new type of modern couple, both of them educated and working cooperatively not only in their family life but professionally. Lou Henry was one of the first women in America to earn a degree in geology.[4] She later collaborated professionally with her husband in many ways, from fieldwork to research and scholarship, notably in coauthoring a monumental anno-

FIGURE 12 Herbert and Lou Henry Hoover at entry of Stanford house, 1928. (Courtesy Hoover Institution Archives)

tated translation of the sixteenth-century mining treatise *De re metallica*, published in 1912.

Lou's willingness to be unconventional and to depart from traditional gender roles expressed itself in other aspects of her life as well, including the house she built for her family. Birge Clark wrote, "The prevailing spirit of the house is one of extreme livableness and utter lack of formality and ostentation, the individuality of the owner being evidenced everywhere by the lack of conventionality and disregard of tradition or the accepted ways of doing things."[5]

Trained in science and engineering, Herbert and Lou exemplified a rational and pragmatic approach toward solving problems. Anne Beiser Allen began her biography of Mrs. Hoover with the following characterization:

> Among those who had worked closely with the Hoovers during the hectic days of World War I, when they organized relief projects for noncombattants in

> Europe and later coordinated food production in the United States to support the war effort, these two inspired an admiration that amounted almost to awe. It seemed that there was no problem that this couple—together or singly—could not handle, from a calm, logical appraisal to a simple, rational solution.[6]

The Hoovers' familiarity with many parts of the non-Western world was also relevant to the design of the Stanford house. Following their marriage, they lived in China, Australia, Burma, and elsewhere; in traveling from these places to London and the United States they visited many other regions, including Japan, New Zealand, Samoa, Ceylon, Egypt, South Africa, as well as many parts of Europe. Everywhere they traveled, Lou, especially, was interested in local cultures and environments—studying geological and topographical conditions with her husband; noting the arts, architecture, and daily life of native populations; and even working diligently on learning to speak and read Chinese during their more than two years' residence in Tientsin.[7] In 1902 she became one of the first members of the National Geographic Society, an organization devoted to exploration and the popular dissemination of information on non-Western regions of the world.[8] In discussing her house in a letter in 1933, Lou said, "I have liked the primitive houses in many lands especially for their simplicity."[9]

To the extent that the Hoover House was influenced by non-Western or "primitive" architecture, it is relevant to ask about the Hoovers' racial attitudes. Both of them shared some of the prejudices common to white Americans of their time, and in her private correspondence Lou occasionally used words such as "Chinamen" and "darkies."[10] Yet, when she saw the designation "Jap's Room" on a floor plan of the house, she wrote to Arthur Clark, telling him to remove it, "for Japanese object so strenuously to that term."[11] (It was removed from the final plans for the house, although it remained on the preliminary plan that Birge Clark later included in his "Memoirs" and is illustrated here as Fig. 4.)[12] A recent study of Herbert Hoover's relationship with African Americans describes the controversy aroused by his desegregation of the Department of Commerce when he headed it in the 1920s, stating, "Despite his limitations and failures in understanding the deeply rooted nature of racism, he came to view himself as a friend of the Negro people and tried to carry that belief into action."[13] It will be argued here that the elements of non-Western architecture found in the Hoover House were motivated not by exoticism or whimsy, as was often the case during that period, but by a genuine admiration for the principles and virtues found in much "primitive" architecture.

Despite the Hoovers' secure position in the conservative world of business and then in government, their personal friends included unconventional writers and artists, such as the feminist Anne Martin and Mary Hunter Austin, author of popular books on the American West and Native Americans.[14] Another of Lou's close friends was the artist and naturalist Mary Vaux Walcott, an advocate of the welfare of Native Americans who lived for long periods on Indian reservations.[15]

Lou had a passion for outdoor life and physical exercise. As a child she had preferred baseball, fishing, and hiking to traditional feminine activities.[16] In college, her attraction to geology was due in part to her love of the vigorous fieldwork involved in it. And she was an accomplished horsewoman: one of her Stanford classmates described her as "an athletic, out-of-doors girl who rode her bronco like a centaur."[17] Throughout her adult life, she promoted athletic activity, especially for girls and women, devoting much of her time to lecturing and writing on the subject for the Girl Scouts organization, in which she held national leadership positions.[18] An article on her in 1928 (as the wife of the presidential candidate), evidently based on an interview, included the following remarks:

> The Scout movement, according to Mrs. Hoover, is "an adventure in comradeship." Let girls, she urges, learn to do what makes for a full life for us all. Let them know something about electrical equipment, carpentering, plumbing. . . . Hiking, campfire building, wood lore give, says Mrs. Hoover, the poise and health that make the young woman equal to the strain of even the most complicated urban life. In this back-to-nature movement, she believes, there should be no clinging vines.[19]

In another interview of 1928, Lou explained the terraced roofs of her house by saying, "I could never see any sense in staying indoors, when all outside is fresh air and sunlight."[20] Even toward the end of her life, in her sixties, Lou took weeklong camping trips on horseback in mountainous country, amazing her companions with her "long hours of riding and sleeping on the ground."[21] Birge Clark, describing the Hoover House in letters of 1928, wrote, "The Hoover family's love of the outdoors was responsible for their desire to have all the rooms opening out on spacious terraces connected with outside stairs," and that the house "is primarily a place for living outdoors."[22] Lou herself said that the main terrace was "where we live a great deal of the time—for nine months of the year it is the family living room" (see Fig. 38).[23] She and her sons reportedly slept on the terraces in hot weather.[24] And she once invited an acquaintance to come to Stanford and "camp with us on the Hill."[25]

The Hoover House was shaped also by Herbert and Lou's love of entertaining. Throughout their lives they enjoyed hosting large dinner parties and other events and having overnight guests. This was no doubt a reason for the large number of rooms on the ground floor that could serve as extra bedrooms. Lou reportedly planned the living room to accommodate theatrical performances, with the large doorway and steps up into the dining room allowing its use as a stage.[26] The Hoovers were known especially for their casual style of entertaining, Lou being adept at handling last-minute changes such as the doubling of the number of guests. Toward the end of her life, when she and Herbert were living in the Waldorf Towers in New York, arriving dinner guests were once surprised to find her under the dining table fixing an electrical problem.[27]

Among the Hoovers' most distinctive character traits were strong ideals of propriety and discretion. In Herbert's case this may have stemmed from his Quaker upbringing; Lou, though not from a Quaker family, had admired Quaker principles since childhood and later called herself a Quaker "by adoption."[28] Their innate modesty made them somewhat uncomfortable with the wealth Herbert had accumulated in his career. (By about 1910, Herbert was telling friends he was tired of making money and wanted to find more significant goals in life.)[29] The distaste they had for ostentation was a factor in the design of their house. It had to be large and comfortable enough to meet their needs as public figures, but they did not want it to appear grandiose. During the design and construction of the house this feeling was compounded by a concern that publicity about the building might prove embarrassing to Herbert's position as administrator of wartime and postwar relief work.

The Hoovers had an intense desire to keep their personal lives private. This was the main reason for Lou's dismissal of the first architect she hired to design the Stanford house, and it caused her to avoid public statements and interviews about the house and her family's life in it. Her desire for privacy was so strong that she routinely burned personal letters and asked family members to do the same.[30] This naturally is frustrating to the historian attempting to understand her thinking and motives. In fact, one of her biographers stated that her "habitual reticence and reluctance to share her inner thoughts and feelings . . . made some observers consider her aloof."[31]

Throughout her life, Lou had a strong personal interest in architecture, to the extent that she once said, "I have often wished that I had time to make a profession of it."[32] Her childhood diaries and other papers reveal a lively interest in buildings. And the scrapbooks she assembled during her years of traveling throughout the world with Herbert reveal her to be a close observer of buildings, especially those of non-Western cultures. Her role in the design of the house at Stanford was her major involvement in architectural design, but her interest in the subject persisted in the following years.[33] In 1922, when Herbert was serving as secretary of commerce, he had an inexpensive demonstration house built in a Washington park, as part of his "Better Homes for America" campaign; when the demonstration ended, Lou took an active interest in what she dubbed the "Little House," raising funds to purchase it for the Girl Scouts organization, move it to a permanent site, and upgrade it.[34]

FIGURE 13 One of Lou Henry Hoover's faculty "cottages," 607 Mayfield Avenue, Stanford. (Norris Pope)

The following year, Lou conceived a project to build small houses on the Stanford campus that could be afforded by young faculty members. Using Birge Clark as the architect, she constructed seven of them, some of which she was able to sell, while she rented and managed the others for a number of years (Fig. 13).[35] Although simple in design, these "cottages" were more conventional than the Hoover House in some respects, especially in having sloping, tiled roofs. Birge Clark later noted that Lou was not closely involved in their actual design, as she was mainly in Washington DC during the period.[36] But she took seriously the challenge of creating well-planned inexpensive housing.

Following Herbert's election to the presidency but before he assumed office, Lou reportedly studied floor plans of the White House, and while living there she took a strong interest in the building and the authentic furnishing of it.[37] But Lou's major architectural project while in the White House was the creation of Rapidan Camp, a weekend retreat for the family in the Blue Ridge Mountains of Virginia. Working with an architect friend, James Rippin, Lou oversaw the design and construction of a group of rustic log and stone cabins, which she furnished with simple furniture and Indian rugs and pottery (Figs. 14–15, and see Fig. 60).[38]

Following the Hoover presidency, Lou continued her interest in architectural matters. According to a letter written by Herbert after her death, she contributed to the design of Hoover Tower, constructed in the late 1930s on the Stanford campus to house the Hoover Institution. Writing to the widow of the building's architect, Arthur Brown, Hoover recalled, "One day when he [Brown] and I were discussing how a tower could fit into the Romanesque motif of the University, Mrs. Hoover suggested he might find justification in the towers of the Cathedral at Salamanca. He at once rejoiced and that is its dome."[39] Comparison of the Hoover Tower with the tower of the sixteenth-century cathedral of

FIGURE 14 Rapidan Camp, Virginia, one of the cabins, c. 1931. (Courtesy Herbert Hoover Presidential Library)

FIGURE 15 Rapidan Camp, interior of President's Cabin, with Lou Henry Hoover and friends, c. 1931. (Courtesy Herbert Hoover Presidential Library)

FIGURE 16 Hoover Tower, Stanford University, constructed c. 1940. (Courtesy Hoover Institution Archives)

FIGURE 17 Cathedral of Salamanca, tower. (*Die Baukunst Spaniens* [Dresden, 1895], vol. 2, detail of plate 82)

Salamanca in Spain shows that Brown simplified greatly the prototype but that the essentials remained similar: a square tower with three arched openings near the top of each side; an octagonal drum, with obelisk-like forms at the corners; a dome; and an elongated lantern at the top (Figs. 16–17).

Lou was not shy about expressing her architectural opinions, at least when she was speaking privately. While visiting the Century of Progress exhibition in Chicago in 1933, she wrote to her son Allan that she found "most of it dreary . . . reminiscent of California highway architecture as practiced by filling stations and hot dog stands."[40]

Lou Henry Hoover's lifelong interest in architecture, her willingness to break with convention, her love of healthy outdoor living, her interest in the non-Western world, and her sense of propriety and modesty, all shaped the house she created for her family at Stanford.

Chapter Two CREATION OF THE HOUSE

From 1902 to 1917 the Hoovers' main residence was in London, where the headquarters of the international mining company in which Herbert was a partner was located. They lived for most of this time in the Red House in Kensington, an old structure set in a garden, which they recalled fondly in later years, and much of whose furnishings were installed in the new house at Stanford (Fig. 18).[1]

The family was frequently on the move, however, to the far-flung parts of the world where Herbert's work took him, and in about 1908 they also began spending periods of time in the United States, gravitating more and more to the environs of their alma mater. In early 1909 they rented the house of a Stanford administrator, where they stayed for a month before moving to New York City. In the following decade, the family moved back and forth from Stanford to New York, Washington, and London with amazing frequency—living successively in at least ten different houses in the Stanford area, most of them in the university's faculty-housing precinct adjacent to the campus (where Herbert was qualified to reside as a member of the university's board of trustees).[2]

Lou and the two Hoover sons, Herbert Jr. and Allan, spent more time in California than did Herbert Sr., whose work kept him mostly on the East Coast and abroad—first with his business affairs, then in his wartime efforts for the relief of Belgium, then as director of the United States Food Administration. But Lou and Herbert shared the desire to create a home at Stanford.

In view of Herbert's burden of work and frequent absences, as well as Lou's strong interest in architecture, it was natural that she took primary responsibility for the planning of their Stanford house. As early as 1912, according to biographer Helen Pryor, "She began sketching her ideas for the permanent home they planned to build on San Juan Hill."[3] This hill, on university land just to the southeast of the Stanford campus, was near several of the Stanford faculty houses the Hoovers rented in the 1910s. A reservoir had been constructed on the hill in about 1907; the road on which the Hoover House was built was first called Reservoir Drive but was renamed Mirada Avenue.[4] The lot acquired by the Hoovers

FIGURE 18 The Red House, London. (Courtesy Hoover Institution Archives)

was about one-and-a-quarter acres, which was later increased with the addition of adjacent property. Like all lots in this Stanford housing area, it was not purchased but rather leased from the university for a yearly ground-rental fee.[5]

In May 1917 Lou telegraphed Herbert, who was in Washington, asking, "Do you think it advisable [to] build fifty thousand dollar house or five thousand or none at all." He replied, "You can build any sort of house you wish but if it is to be the ultimate family headquarters it should be substantial and roomy. The cost is secondary."[6]

To design the house, Lou in mid-1917 chose the San Francisco architect Louis Christian Mullgardt, who at that time was building the Stanford president's house (later called the Knoll and now used by the Music Department), into which President Ray Lyman Wilbur and his family moved, the following year (Fig. 19).[7] Lou's choice of Mullgardt is puzzling, since much of his work, including the Knoll, featured elaborate and unusual ornament (Birge Clark later called the style "Portuguese Gothic"), very different from the stark forms of the house the Hoovers eventually built.[8] Mullgardt's two best-known works at that time, the Court of Abundance at the 1914–15 Panama-Pacific Exposition in San Francisco and the DeYoung Museum in that city's Golden Gate Park, also had abundant eclectic

FIGURE 19 President's House, Stanford University (now the Knoll), constructed 1918, designed by Louis Christian Mullgardt. (Courtesy Stanford University Archives)

ornamentation.[9] This suggests that Lou did not yet have a clear idea of what she wanted. But she soon began formulating her concepts.

For the Hoovers, Mullgardt produced a design for a long, two-storey house on the San Juan Hill site—a perspective rendering of which was published in the journal *Architect and Engineer* in December 1917 (Fig. 20).[10] It shows a structure somewhat similar to the final house, in its extended configuration on the hillside, but longer and more conventional in some respects, especially in having sloping, tiled roofs. The October issue of *Architect and Engineer* had contained some information about the design, in an article on Mullgardt's work; it said that the architect was "preparing plans for an elaborate country house for Mr. Herbert C. Hoover . . . [which] in design will be what Mr. Mullgardt styles the American school. Fireproof material will be used, with an exterior of white cement and terra cotta tile roof."[11]

But by the time the drawing was published, Lou had fired Mullgardt, angered by his indiscretion in trumpeting the project to the press. Besides the item in *Architect and Engineer*, there had been a story in the *San Francisco Examiner*, October 13, 1917 (subsequently picked up by the national wire services), entitled "Hoover Plans $50,000 Home, Food Administrator Having Louis Mullgardt Draft Building Near Stanford University":

> Herbert C. Hoover, United States Food Administrator at Washington, will take up his residence in California, it was announced yesterday, on the completion of

FIGURE 20 "Residence for Mr. and Mrs. Herbert C. Hoover," design by Louis Christian Mullgardt, 1917. (*The Architect and Engineer*, December 1917, 99)

a country home near Stanford University, for which plans are now being made by Louis Christian Mullgardt. . . . Mullgardt, who was the architect of the Court of Abundance at the Panama-Pacific Exposition, said yesterday: "The Hoover residence will be completed in about one year. It will contain twenty-one rooms and will be two stories high. The structure will cost approximately $50,000. It will have a white cement facing and will be purely California in style."[12]

Besides the Hoovers' inherent desire for privacy, Lou was distressed by any publicity that might damage her husband's reputation in wartime. Emphasis on the large size and cost of the house was especially galling. Lou wrote a letter to the family's legal and financial advisor, Curtis H. Lindley, describing her troubled relationship with Mullgardt.[13] The letter also reveals some of her attitudes about the house she wished to build.

> I want to be extricated from a folly. . . . I engaged Christian Mullgardt to make preliminary plans for "a small house" for me, to harmonize with the University residential architecture,—yet not to be like it. The smallness and unostentation thereof being its strongest features [Lou's emphasis]. And the understanding was that I might never build it,—and almost certainly would not till "after the war". . . . He turned out a sketch which I quite liked,—but for the fact that it was extremely big! And a very rough estimate of its cost was $40,000—which he acknowledged might easily extend to $50,000! . . . Meantime, without consultation with or permission from me, he published in a journal of architecture . . . this sketch [evidently the drawing in *Architect and Engineer*].

Lou proceeded to describe to Lindley the embarrassing and unjust publicity to which she felt her husband was being subjected, noting, "It does not happen to be anyone else's business whether the Food Administrator should build a house of half a million dollars or more,—nor where nor when. We can and had settled such a matter with our own conscience by deciding it was an improper thing to do." She continued the story of her dealings with Mullgardt, relating that he had apologized for the publicity but claimed it wasn't his fault; that she had written to him that "the building of a cottage" would have to be postponed due to the war; that she had asked him to "send me his account to date"; and that he had submitted an inflated bill for $2,400.

Lou pointed out that Mullgardt had received a good deal of "advertisement" from the design, while the work was now useless to her, as she could not "live in a house whose detail, whether incorrect or not, had been studied and gossiped about over the whole countryside." She asked Lindley several questions about "professional etiquette" in architecture, saying, "I may be influenced by my miner's training. I feel that my engineer's report is my report. Perhaps the architect's is the world's." And she concluded, "If you think the wisest thing to do is just to pay the $2400, and have learned a lesson to stay away from architects,—will you have your firm pay it as soon as possible, and send the full account on to me?"

No doubt because of this unpleasantness, and also because she was now thinking more critically about the kind of house she wanted, Lou put the project on hold. In 1918 she purchased a faculty residence close to the San Juan Hill site, in which the family was to live until the new house was completed in mid-1920.[14] When she returned to her project, in late 1918, she took a very different approach to the use of architects. Rather than go to another well-known professional, she enlisted the help of a friend and neighbor, Arthur Bridgman Clark, whose discretion she could trust completely, and who would give her the major role in producing the design.[15]

FIGURE 21 Clark House, 618 Mirada Avenue, Stanford, designed by Arthur B. Clark, 1909. (Author)

Clark was the head of the Art Department at Stanford (he had been the first instructor in art at the university, when Herbert and Lou were students), had been trained as an architect, and had designed several houses in the Stanford area, including his own (Fig. 21).[16] The two families were close; the Hoovers had even entrusted their son Herbert Jr. to the care of the Clarks for about a year when they were in England overseeing Belgian relief at the beginning of the war.[17] And they were neighbors, the Clarks' home being close to the house in which the Hoovers lived from 1918 to 1920.[18]

Lou had, in fact, already consulted Professor Clark regarding her plans for a house. Her papers contain a letter from him, of September 27, 1917, responding to questions she had posed about Mullgardt's design.[19] Although Lou's letter does not survive, Clark's reply sheds light on her concerns, as well as on the architectural preferences of Clark himself.

> Dear Mrs. Hoover!-
>
> Your letter about the new house came yesterday morning and I thought quite a bit about the problem during the day, and walked by the lot a couple of times before seeing the architect's plan [that is, Mullgardt's design]. . . . It is a masterpiece of design and adaptation to a particular site, in my humble opinion. . . . It is on the upper side, the wide veranda makes a step which will disguise the fact that the building is two stories high, vines and shrubbery can completely conceal the veranda wall, except for actual windows, and the bending wall

> [Clark sketched part of the plan here] with the slight bays helps again to make it rambling and unpretentious.
>
> Of course 165 feet seems enormous, compared with any other house on San Juan Hill . . . [but] Mr. Mullgardt's design will look smaller than it really is, on account of its low eave line. . . . It seems he has handled it very skillfully to keep it unpretentious. . . . I think you should have no concern on that score. [Lou disagreed, judging from her letter to Lindley.]

Clark commented on the interior of Mullgardt's proposed house, noting that the rooms were large and could be reduced in size if Lou wanted the overall house to be shorter; but he added, "people who insist on making the whole world their friends, I suppose do need large rooms to receive them in." Regarding the exterior, he suggested adding a "modest gable above the living room," which "would help the design by giving a central accent, a point of rest on the long horizontal line." This enthusiasm of Clark's for conventional roofs adds to the evidence that the stark, cubic, flat-roofed form of the Hoover House as it was built was conceived by the Hoovers, not by their architects.

Lou had evidently asked Clark about making the house fireproof, for he spoke of the use of concrete for this purpose, as well as mentioning "interlocking tile." He also answered questions she had posed about the "present availability of men for building" and the cost of construction. He expressed gratitude "that you think my opinions worth having," reported news of his children, hoped that "the house may materialize soon and bring the Hoovers back here," and added a postscript saying he was sending "a blueprint of some plans I have been collecting during the summer."

It may have been this exchange that gave Lou the idea of using Clark as her architect. He was trustworthy, knowledgeable about local building conditions, and concerned primarily with the Hoovers' needs and desires. In a letter to Lou, following her request that he do the work, he wrote, "My idea of this architectural job is that it is not on a percentage basis but that you are the architect-in-chief—and that I am a sort of architectural 'secretary,' while Mr. Davis does the heavy work. Such an arrangement will accomplish the results you want, I think."[20] And when Clark illustrated the completed house in his book *Art Principles in House, Furniture, and Village Building* in 1921 (see Figs. 42–43), he identified himself as the architect but noted that "Mrs. Lou Henry Hoover contributed the best ideas, while Charles T. Davis and Birge M. Clark carried them out."[21]

Birge Clark, Arthur Clark's eldest son, later provided the most detailed information about the design and execution of the house. Born in 1893, Birge graduated from Stanford in 1914, received an architectural degree from Columbia University in 1917, served in the Air Force in France from late 1917 to the beginning of 1919, and returned to Stanford in February or March of 1919 to assist in the design of the Hoovers' house.[22] He went on to a successful career as an architect in the Palo Alto area. Especially in the later years of his long life (he lived to the age of ninety-six), he produced memoirs and other accounts of his work on the Hoover House.[23]

According to Birge, his father had been reluctant to take on the design of such a large house, as it would interfere with his university responsibilities, but he finally agreed, "[telling] Mrs. Hoover that she could act as the architect and he would obtain a draftsman and correlate the design work," as well as anticipating the assistance of Birge when he returned home from the war.[24]

The "draftsman" was Charles Davis, who had worked for several San Francisco architects, notably Willis Polk, and had assisted in the design of lavish houses such as Filoli, the Georgian-style mansion near Stanford built for William Bourn in 1916.[25] Especially in the early stages of the Hoover House design, before Birge joined the team, Davis played a central role in the project. In one of Arthur Clark's letters to Lou, he wrote, "Here are the plans and elevations. . . . The plans you may mark in any way you like as Mr. Davis has all the data on other sheets. He has straightened the main stair feeling it will be safer if encountered in the dark. . . . Mr. Davis would like the Elevations—not necessarily the floor plans—on Monday."[26]

Birge recalled that when "I returned in March, the exterior of the house had been pretty well settled, as was the general plan," and it was mainly the interior that remained to be designed.[27] Davis was "doing the major part of the work. . . . I went to work under him and when the building started I acted more or less as an inspector and general architectural factotum, and since Mrs. Hoover had known me well, probably more or less as messenger boy between her, Davis, and my father."[28]

Birge wrote that he and Davis "made the drawings for the house, other than the structural drawings which were designed by structural engineer T. Ronneberg."[29] And he noted that Davis "was quite in awe of Mrs. Hoover, whom he regarded very highly, and frequently said she was a unique client in all his experience."[30] In another of his accounts, Birge wrote, "Mrs. Hoover really did act as the architect and Davis and I were draftsmen, though my father, in whose ideas Mrs. Hoover had great confidence, lent a hand from time to time."[31] Birge also recalled that an early design of the house showed the living-room terraces with a curving form, which Mrs. Hoover "ruled out" as being "too much in the grand manner," and that "she would occasionally tease Davis by saying 'that looks like a house for William Bourn.'"[32]

These recollections by Birge Clark add to the evidence that Lou was in effect the architect of the house—that is, that she made all the important decisions about its design, relying on her hired professionals mainly for their technical expertise and to produce drawings following her directions. Moreover, Lou's private secretary, Dare Stark, reported in a letter of February 1919, "The lady [Lou's nickname with her staff] is occupied these days correcting Mr. Clark's plans of the new house every time he draws them."[33] And Herbert, in a telegram to Lou on April 22, 1919, stated, "Build house as you planned it yourself. Probably won't use it much for 15 years, but want it right then."[34] (The suggestion here that Lou had "planned" the house at an earlier time is puzzling, but it was repeated by Herbert many years later, when he wrote in his memoirs, regarding the house, "She had leased the lot some years before, and, upon our return to California, she resurrected her preliminary architectural drawings and began to build.")[35]

Lou's dominant role in the design is indicated also by the fact that its most distinctive characteristics, stark cubic forms and flat roofs, are not found in the other houses designed by Arthur Clark, nor in the buildings Charles Davis is likely to have worked on (as draftsman for Willis Polk), nor in the great majority of the buildings Birge Clark went on to design—although Birge could not have contributed, in any case, to the overall form of the Hoover House since it was essentially designed by the time he joined the team.

Another possible contributor to the design, however, must be considered: Herbert Hoover. Birge Clark, in his written accounts and interviews toward the end of his life, frequently stated or implied that Herbert had little interest in the house, his only demand being that it be fireproof, which resulted in the choice of reinforced concrete as the structural material.[36] This impression of Herbert's indifference is given also by the stories of his jocular remarks about the house. Clark recounted, for example, that on one of Herbert's infrequent visits to Stanford while the house was being designed, Lou showed him some sketches, but "he seemed only mildly interested and looked out the window and said 'I really don't care what it looks like just so it doesn't look like that insane asylum of Wilbur's over there'"—referring to the Stanford president's house designed by Mullgardt.[37]

But other accounts by Birge Clark, less well known, suggest that Herbert did have ideas about the house that shaped its design, besides fireproof construction. In an interview in 1950, Clark recalled that Herbert had "three requirements—[the house] must have a view and the roofs must be useful, and it must be fireproof." Since the usefulness of the roofs required their being flat, this distinctive aspect of the house may have been due primarily to Herbert. Lou, however, concurred and was enthusiastic about the idea. She reportedly considered putting a tennis court or a swimming pool on one of the terraces.[38] And when asked about her house in an interview in 1928, she emphasized that the roofs were flat and said, "Fortunately our architect was an understanding person [and] let me have everything my own way. . . . So I arranged for all the rooms we needed . . . and gave my real attention to the roof."[39]

Birge Clark also implied Herbert's role in the design when he wrote, "Neither Mr. or Mrs. Hoover wanted the house to be related to any historical style," and he later amplified the point by saying, "Neither of them wanted the house to be a French Provincial, an English manor, early California, or any historical style."[40] In the early years of the twentieth century the rejection of traditional precedent in architecture was still a remarkable notion. It was not a position that would have been taken by someone truly indifferent to the appearance of a building.

In one of his interviews, Clark also recalled that Herbert had said the house "should look as if a child had piled up blocks."[41] This odd remark reveals an attraction to simple, cubic forms in architecture that was certainly not common in 1919, and it suggests that Herbert had a hand in giving the house its distinctive cubist appearance. It may be noted that an interest in children's blocks, as inspiration for architectural form, appeared elsewhere in avant-garde modernism of the period, for example in Frank Lloyd Wright's assertion that his own work had been shaped by his childhood exposure to the Froebel educational system, which employed cubic blocks and other primary forms.[42]

In light of the fact that Herbert later said the house was intended to be "a Hopi house"—the most categorical association of the house with Pueblo architecture by either of the Hoovers—it seems likely that Herbert did play a role in the shaping of the building, even if he sometimes masked this role with jocularity or feigned indifference. His genuine interest in the project is suggested also by a cable he sent to Lou from Paris in January 1919: "Hope you start building University house at once."[43]

Regardless of the extent of Herbert's contribution, it clearly was Lou who produced the actual design of the house. Her intense participation in the process was later documented in detail by Birge Clark, for example in this description of their working relationship:

> This studio [a room in the Clark house] was converted into a drafting room and was just . . . big enough for two drafting tables for Davis and me, and a table on which we could study drawings when Mrs. Hoover came over, which she did frequently, and mostly unannounced. Mrs. Hoover was always delighted to climb up on a stool and look at whatever we were working on, and just as we would lay a piece of tracing paper over a drawing and make a freehand suggestion or alteration, she was delighted to do this also. She was exceedingly diplomatic in her criticisms, and usually started with praise of whatever we were doing, and if she did agree with it was delighted; if she didn't, she was careful to say that our way was probably a good way, but what she had in mind was something a little different. Like many people, she knew what she didn't like, but had trouble in

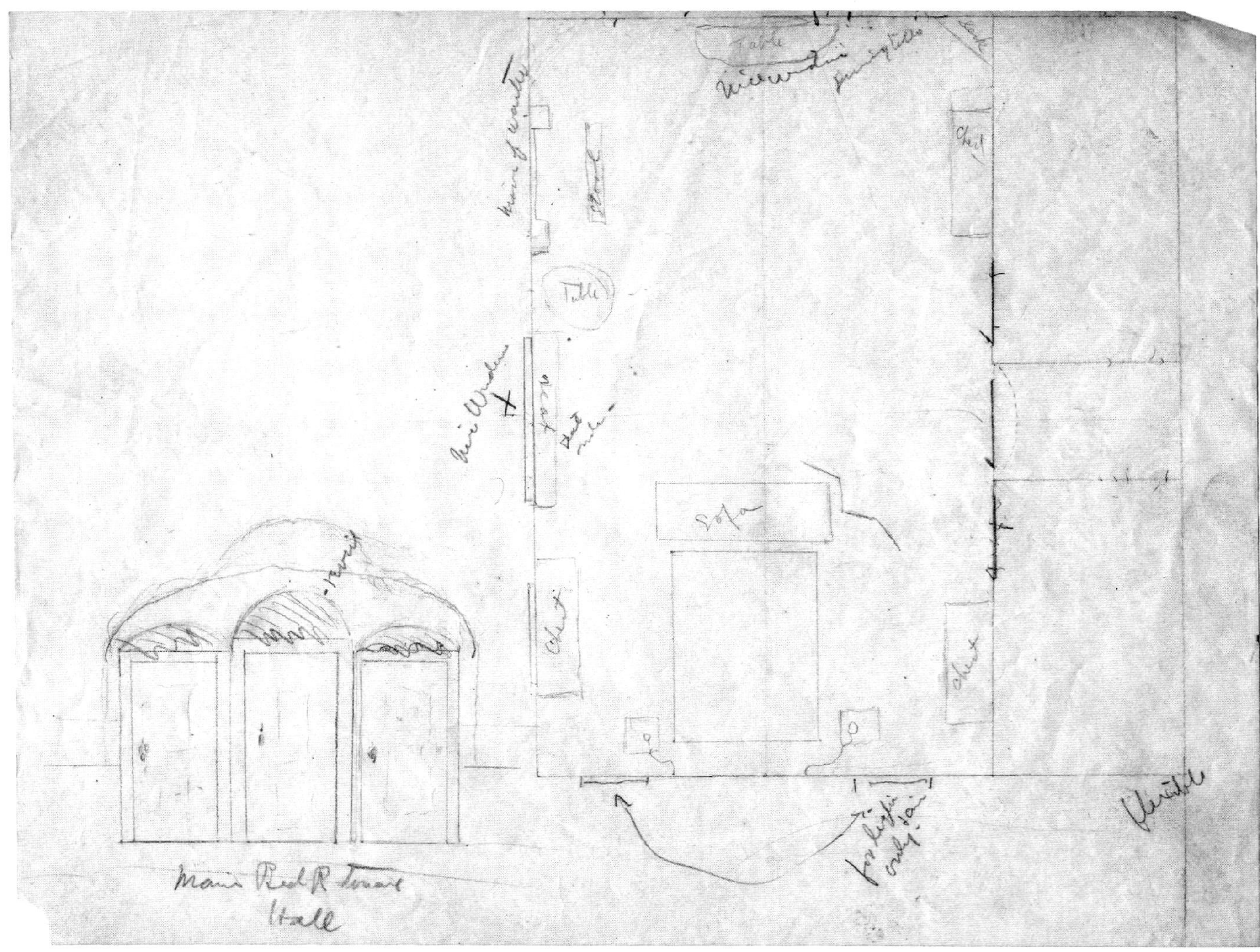

FIGURE 22 Drawing by Lou Henry Hoover with floor plan and section drawing of bedroom. (Courtesy Stanford University Archives)

knowing in advance what she would like. Her sketches were not only of floor or room plans; sometimes she would make little elevations of how she hoped the end or side of a room would look. Sometimes she would mail us these, and since they were sketched from memory . . . we weren't always sure whether she meant something more than was intended.[44]

Birge Clark preserved some of these sketches drawn by Lou.[45] One of them, to which he referred following the passage above, shows a floor plan of the master bedroom and a section drawing through the room (Fig. 22). Describing it, Birge wrote, "We thought maybe she was indicating a vaulted ceiling, and sent

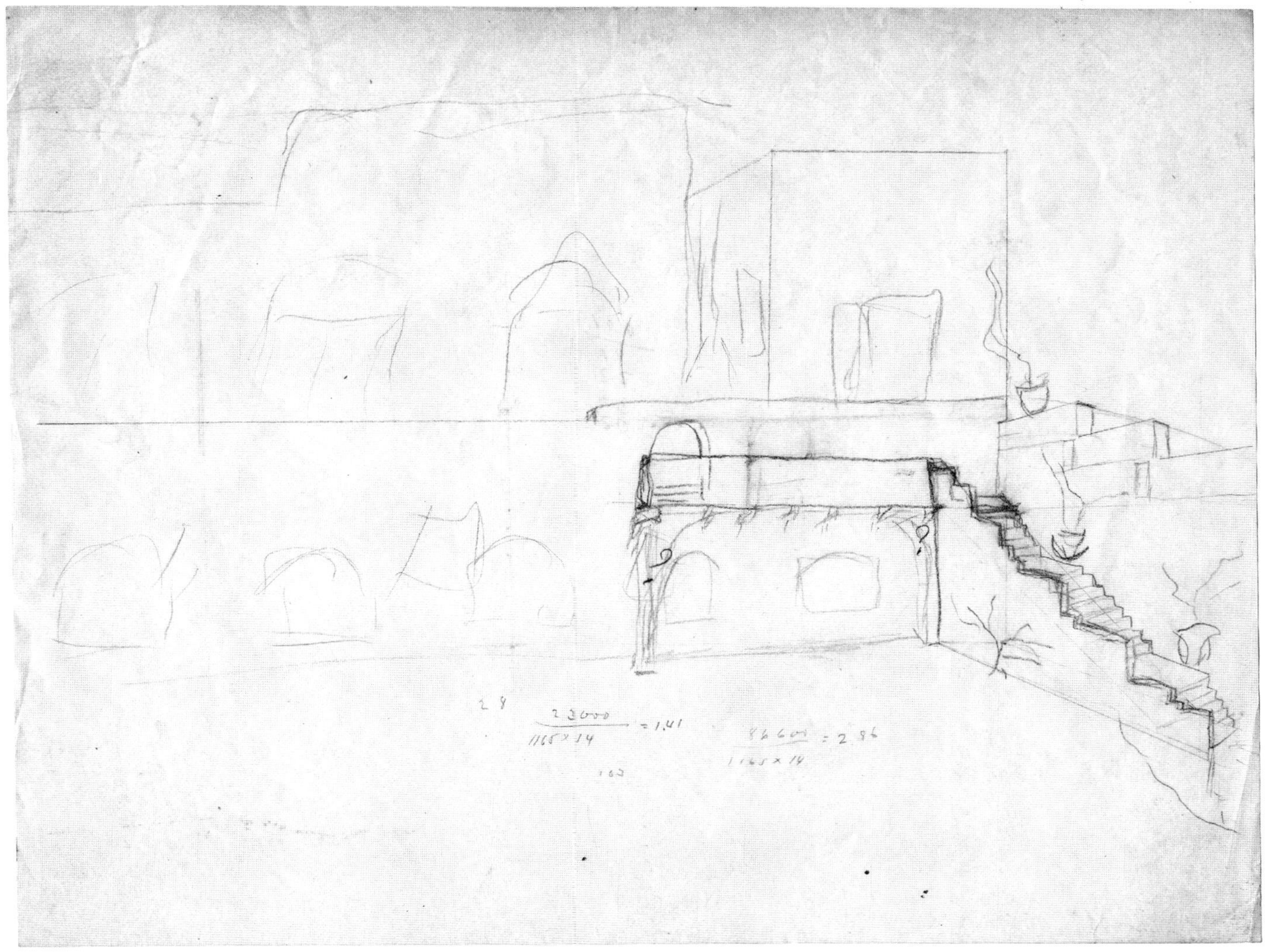

off a letter asking about this, and presently received a vigorous negative, saying it was only her poor sketching from memory and was meant to show the coves at the corners of the walls and ceiling."[46] Lou's drawings are somewhat amateurish but they reveal careful thought and an ability to conceptualize rather complex forms and spaces. They range from floor plans to elevations, sections, and perspectives, and often include both drafted and sketched lines in the same drawing (Figs. 22–24, and see Fig. 31).

FIGURE 23 Drawing by Lou Henry Hoover of garden side of house. (Courtesy Stanford University Archives)

The involvement of Mrs. Hoover described by Birge Clark took place rather late in the design process, for the overall planning and exterior design of the

FIGURE 24 Drawing by Lou Henry Hoover with perspective and section drawing of living room. (Courtesy Stanford University Archives)

house had largely occurred before Birge returned home. But Lou had been actively engaged in the earlier stages of the design, too. This is shown, for example, by a letter she wrote to Arthur Clark, which is undated but must be from the preliminary design phase, when the basic floor plan and shape of the house were being worked out.[47] This document reveals Lou's ability to visualize architectural forms and details in her mind and to describe them as if they had already been constructed. The letter is worth quoting in full.

> Dear Professor Clark,
>
> I have been living most of the day in the front of the downstairs part of my house. Have even got it mostly furnished! Am enclosing my suggestions.[48] I have not gone to the outside yet,—(except just at the corner of the wall) but I dont [*sic*] quite see how all the windows those rooms must have are going to look nice on the outside!

> Why can't we make a little stair climbing up the inside of that wall in some way? And if it would bring people out just where we dont want them, we might let them saunter along as far as necessary on a tiny balcony outside the veranda parapet? If their heads are going to look funny above the parapet, we could raise the latter for a few feet in length there? They could either just walk in through a break in the same parapet, or have a little door like the one there used to be on the little stair which came up the middle of the veranda. [This must refer to an earlier stage of the planning.]

Lou's concern for the relationship of stairs, walls, and parapets is seen in one of her drawings that was preserved by Birge Clark (Fig. 23).[49] Her letter continues:

> Do you know, I believe with the thing developing as it is now, it is going to look better from this side if it goes straight across instead of curving? And the rooms will group better too! [This must refer to the shape of the ground floor and main terrace on the garden side of the house.][50]
>
> If you have any new outside sketches to spare, please send them along to me. And a plan of the main floor,—I find I haven't any now.
>
> Hoping the knee is very much better,—
>
> Sincerely,
> Lou Henry Hoover

Lou's enthusiasm for visualizing and designing the house on the site led her to devise an unusual method of working. Birge Clark described it in his 1969 memoir:

> When I first returned [in February or March 1919], a platform scaffold about 30-feet long and 10-feet high had been erected in the middle of the site. There was also a horizontal platform leading out from the reservoir road [the approach to the house, later Mirada Avenue] to this scaffold and there was a chair on each. This was done so that Mrs. Hoover could be sure of just what views could be seen, seated from the living room and dining room windows, as well as from the terrace. [Clark then describes the views at that time, before the surrounding trees were as tall as they later became.] Mrs. Hoover loved these views and frequently told people to go up to the highest deck, and they would protest to me afterwards that the steep steps had terrified them.[51]

Since a viewing platform of this sort is hardly a common device in architectural design, it was no doubt conceived by Lou herself, and it shows the importance she placed on the relationship between the house and its natural environment. This is seen also in remarks she later included in a letter:

> We wished to put the house almost at the top of a considerable hill on a decidedly sloping piece of ground because of the views to be obtained there. We established

> the level of the main floor where it could be easily reached from the road and where an excellent view could be obtained over the valley from the opposite side as one walked through the house. While from the floor above, the view extended also in the other direction to the distant mountains over the brow of this hill on which it stands.[52]

Lou's desire to maximize the views from the house led her to reject the use of window drapes. In the same letter as above, she wrote, "The views from these windows [in the dining and living rooms] are very beautiful. . . . I have never found a hanging that would not detract from the beauty of the scene. So I have never had any there."[53]

Besides the viewing platform, another aid used in the design process was a plasticine or clay model, which could be manipulated in order to study the overall massing of the house. The elder Clark suggested making such a model in a letter he wrote to Lou early in the design process.[54] Birge Clark later remembered it as "a plasticene [*sic*] model of the house [with which] we would try out the various bay windows, projecting balconies, outside stairs, etc. . . . It was generally kept on a high cabinet so that it had to be seen from eye level or below as would be the case with the house. In addition, my father occasionally photographed it, which contributed a considerable realism."[55]

One of these photographs has survived (Fig. 25).[56] It shows the house largely as it was built, but with some differences in proportion (for example, the wing housing Herbert's office is smaller in the model) and many differences in fenestration: the living-room windows are arched, and there are small-paned windows in Herbert's office, rather than the large plate-glass windows that were eventually installed.

The aesthetic evaluation of massing and proportions, for which this model was used, was clearly an important consideration in the design—disproof of the assertion sometimes made that the house was planned from a purely functional point of view. In fact, some elements were added to the design despite the fact that they had no function at all. Birge Clark acknowledged this purely visual component, recalling:

> [Mrs. Hoover] did have great concern that the exterior elevations should be good looking. The front elevation on Reservoir Drive [Mirada Avenue] was the subject of many trials. The imitation water spout in the upper-right-hand corner [Fig. 26] was felt to be necessary as a sort of balance at that corner, because of the large stair window; equally, the steps on the second floor roof near the stair window have no functional purpose and were strictly aesthetic elements.[57]

These "steps" at the roofline of the entry side of the house are not only functionless but potentially fatal to someone strolling on the terrace who might think

FIGURE 25 Photograph of plasticine model used in design of Hoover House, 1919. (Courtesy Stanford University Archives)

they are real stairs (see Figs. 46–47). Mrs. Hoover must simply have liked the look of them. (A possible source of this unusual feature will be suggested in the next chapter.)

In mid-June 1919 the laying of the foundations began, even though much of the design was not complete, especially that of the interior. Eleven-year-old Allan Hoover wrote a letter to his father on June 17, reporting on airplanes and a baseball game, asking for Belgian stamps, and adding, "The foundations of our new house are beginning on next Thursday thats in two days."[58]

Judging from the correspondence that has survived, Birge Clark by this time had taken over his father's role of overseeing the project and of being the main vehicle of communication with Lou. Since she was often in New York or Washington or abroad, much of this communication was by letter or telegram, and the resulting misunderstandings and delayed responses sometimes created problems.

The focus now was on the interior planning of the house, to which Lou devoted as much attention as she had done with the exterior, making sketches of her ideas for the detailing of the rooms, and planning the furnishings. In contrast to the innovative character of the exterior, however, the interior was eclectic and drew on more conventional traditions (Figs. 27 and 29, and see Fig. 37). The rooms evoked previous homes of the Hoovers, especially the Red House in London. Much of the furniture from the London house was in fact shipped to San Francisco and put in storage until the Stanford house was ready for it, and Lou even arranged for a fireplace to be removed from the Red House and installed in

FIGURE 26 Hoover House, detail of entrance façade showing "water spout." (Norris Pope)

the new building, although she changed her mind when it arrived and it was never used.[59] The wood-paneled walls in the new house were similar to those in the Red House; Lou later wrote, "Both my husband and I are very fond of panelled walls, so that the living room walls are in a very soft shade of natural oak."[60]

Lou's planning of the interior even affected the exterior to some extent, for example by introducing two "oriel" windows at the southeastern end of the house, (one of which is seen in Fig. 28). She discussed these windows in a letter to Birge

FIGURE 27 Hoover House, living room, 1920s. (Courtesy Hoover Institution Archives)

Clark from Paris, in August 1919, which also suggests how much her planning of the interior was influenced by European models:

> I want to do something to those two little windows . . . the one in the dining-room and the other in the pantry. They haven't quite enough character either outside or in and I felt . . . they would perhaps be better if they were a little oriel with heavy cement frames. . . . I will try to make a rough sketch more or less of my idea, for Mr. Davis' amusement! . . . I have just been staying at an English house where the dining-room, exceedingly like ours, had these end windows all finished in stone.[61]

FIGURE 28 Hoover House, east corner of house, with oriel and bay windows. (Norris Pope)

In regard to the glazing of the windows in the house, Lou and Herbert had conflicting preferences. Birge Clark described the disagreement:

> Mrs. Hoover loved leaded glass windows, and although they were not too easy to see through, all of the dining room and living room windows are of leaded glass. She said people could go outdoors if they wanted to get the detailed view. Leaded glass windows were an anachronism even then, and there were very few mechanics who knew how to make them. Mr. Hoover, however, said he wanted plate glass, and the large plate glass windows in his study are the only windows of this type in the house.[62]

FIGURE 29 Hoover House, Herbert's study, probably 1920s. (Courtesy Stanford University Archives)

Because of these plate-glass windows, Herbert's study creates a somewhat more "modern" impression than other rooms in the house, and this may indicate a more avant-garde outlook on Herbert's part (see Fig. 29). It also underscores his dictum that the house "must have a view." Lou's willingness to let her attraction to traditional windows compromise her love of views underscores her paramount interest in living outdoors, on the terraces—a preference she stated frequently in her letters and interviews. Her desire to spend much of her time outside is seen also in her decision to have a large fireplace on the main terrace, off the living room (Fig. 30, and see Fig. 38).

FIGURE 30 Hoover House, terrace on garden side, with fireplace, 1920s or 1930s. (Courtesy Hoover Institution Archives)

As for the furnishings in the house, Lou later noted that "they are of no period. We have wandered around the world and lived for short periods in many countries on four continents. . . . Thus as one looks at the living room, one sees China, Japan, England, Belgium and various other Oriental and European countries represented."[63]

Lou attempted to give each room an individual character. For the living room she devised a coved ceiling that produced indirect lighting from bulbs recessed in the cove—a relatively new form of lighting at that time (see Fig. 27). And she decided to use the narrow "alcove" room, which opened off the living room, to display some of the gifts Herbert had received in gratitude for his food-relief assistance to the Belgian people during the First World War. She wrote to the Belgian architect Victor Horta, with whom she was apparently acquainted, with the following idea:

> We have an alcove . . . which I am going to arrange to contain the many interesting, beautiful and historic treasures that my husband has from Belgium. And it has just occurred to me that it would be so fitting if they were housed in a semblance of an old Flemish room. So I wanted to ask you to design the panelling of the room for me, along the old Flemish lines.[64]

It is not clear whether Lou understood Horta's importance as an architectural innovator and a creator of the Art Nouveau movement around 1900. That she would ask him to design old Flemish paneling for her alcove suggests she did not. However, the Belgian people and government were so grateful to Herbert Hoover for helping to save the nation from starvation, that Horta, like other distinguished Belgians, may have offered his services carte-blanche to the Hoovers. In any case, nothing seems to have come of Lou's proposal, even though she subsequently wrote two more letters to Horta.[65]

Lou gave particular attention to her own study, on the top floor of the house, entered from the stairway that also led to the Hoover sons' bedrooms. Birge Clark later said that this study was called a "secret room," and that "when she was in [it], she was theoretically out of the house and no one should know where she was. She had her writing desk in front of the three little windows that look out on Reservoir Drive and at the entrance, so if she saw someone coming whom she wanted to see, she could run downstairs. . . . Otherwise a servant would merely say that Mrs. Hoover was out."[66] A flight of narrow "secret stairs" led from this study down to Lou's dressing room adjacent to the master bedroom. A sheet of drawings by Lou includes a floor plan of what must be this study (although with a simpler shape), with sketches of the furniture in it, as well as separate designs for a storage cabinet and a "small step ladder for reaching supplies in cabinet."[67]

On Herbert's occasional visits to the house during the planning and execution of the interior, he continued to play the role of disinterested joker. Birge Clark recalled a particular instance:

> I know Mr. Hoover liked the house because he told me so, but I never heard him express any great delight in it. At the time when the cove living room ceiling had been finished and was being painted, he arrived home, and Mrs. Hoover asked me to come over and meet them both at the house. . . . The second story ceiling over the stair hall had just been "glazed" with an "antique finish." This was the last of several experiments and Mrs. Hoover had thought it was just about right. Mr. Hoover looked at it and said, "Well, I saw some basements in Belgium that looked worse than that," so Mrs. Hoover said, "We won't antique anything from here on." Then she told him about the living room ceiling and how it was attaining a soft general light without any visible source. Mr. Hoover smiled again and said, "Well, it looks kind of like early Pullman to me." This was the only time that I ever saw Mrs. Hoover express any irritableness with her husband. "Bert, it does not," and later that day she phoned me just to say that "Mr. Hoover was merely making a little joke to tease me and he really thought the living room ceiling was just fine." I am sure this was the case, as while Mr. Hoover had a rather dry, though gentle and kind

> sense of humor, I never heard him say anything which would really hurt anyone's feelings, although this time he certainly irritated his wife.[68]

Lou's extensive correspondence with Birge Clark and others provides many examples of her remarkable attention to detail in designing the house. Typical is a passage in a letter she wrote (from Washington DC) to a tradesman in February 1920, regarding sample hardware she had received:

> From the one door handle on the small piece of wood I should think the color scheme very good, although I fancy it would be better still if the metal were considerably darker. Of course it is difficult to tell with such a small surface. . . . It certainly looks much better than anything we saw while in California.[69]

There was a great amount of correspondence between Lou and Birge Clark while the house was in construction in 1920, since Lou during this period was on the move even more frequently than usual, traveling back and forth across the country to be with Herbert as much as possible but still to attend to her affairs in California.[70] One of the topics of this correspondence was the question of how to finish the surfaces of the roof terraces. The original intention was to lay tile in cement, and Lou devoted a lot of effort to looking for appropriate kinds of tiles, from Europe as well as America.[71] But eventually a decision was made to use brick rather than tile.

Choosing the right colors, both outside and inside the house, was very important to Lou. Birge Clark later recalled that she was "particularly concerned that nothing too bright or inharmonious creep in."[72] For the surfaces of the main rooms, she conducted research on how to achieve certain effects of hue, tone, and texture. She focused especially in getting the result she wanted for the upper walls and ceiling of the living room; when it was finished she described it as having "a very soft, old, pale gold" color.[73] (This was apparently the "antiqued" surface that Herbert described as looking like "some basements in Belgium.") Several years later, she wrote that the living-room walls were "in a very soft shade of natural oak, with a little rough plaster in the same shade with just enough gold hidden in it to give it life."[74]

Lou gave special attention to the color of the exterior of the building. The walls were to be left unpainted, with the color being "integral" to the plaster stucco that was troweled over the surface. Before this was done, Lou gave several descriptions of the color she envisioned, once referring to "a very dark cream or pale buff color," another time calling it simply "light," and noting that Herbert had suggested a two-tone scheme, with the upper part of the building light and the bottom storey on the garden side dark.[75]

Experimentation led to the precise proportions of ochre and red pigments that were added to the white cement as the plaster was mixed in batches. When it was applied, Birge reported to Lou (who was then in New York) that it "could be best described [as] a light cream . . . in some lights, sometimes it has a yellow cast and sometimes is merely a warm light grey. We like it very much indeed."[76] When the job was done and Lou saw the garden side of the house one morning, she was distressed that it looked pinkish in color; it turned out that this effect was created by early-morning sunlight reflecting from one of the brick terraces onto the wall.[77] In 1933 Lou described the plaster surface of the house as having "a soft cream color."[78]

Sometime later, however, the surface of the house was painted. Birge Clark in 1969 recalled that the "original stucco was a considerably darker, warmer off-white than the present paint, and since it was unpainted, when wet would show 'wet' colors. This can be seen in the picture of the front of the house the night Hoover was elected, as there had been rain" (see Fig. 36).[79]

Once the building was largely completed, Lou turned some of her attention to the landscaping of the grounds. Her letters to Birge Clark in 1920 and 1921 speak of proposed plantings and the location of the swimming pool, and sometimes include sketches by her, such as one showing patterns of landscaping around the entrance to the house on the entry side.[80] Another drawing is a design for a pergola, supported by columns and shown stepping down the hill (Fig. 31).[81] At least part of this structure was constructed and is seen in early photographs (Fig. 32, and see Fig. 10).[82]

Clark later noted that Lou did not employ a professional landscape designer, just as she felt that no interior decorator was needed.[83] A prominent Bay Area landscapist was recommended to her, but she said "he always made things very large and formal" and thought she and Birge could do it themselves.

The grounds were smaller than they are today, as another property—that of Ellwood Cubberley, dean of the School of Education—occupied part of the present-day garden area to the northeast of the house.[84] In early 1920, Lou wrote to Birge, "Strictly confidentially, I have always kept my eye on the Cubberly [*sic*] house with the idea that sometime it could be moved. Then the garden scheme would be complete with the swimming pool in the Cubberly cellar."[85] She had written to the Cubberleys, proposing a purchase of their property, but she later had to report to Birge that they had replied that "they could not possibly think of giving up their house for any other"—although they offered to give her "first chance" if they were to leave Stanford.[86] As a result, Lou's preferred location for the swimming pool had to give way to a spot adjacent to the east corner of the house.

In mid-June of 1920, Arthur Clark reported to Lou, who was then in New York, that the building was complete except for some interior details, and that the scaffolding had been removed from the exterior.[87] The house was largely ready to be occupied (Figs. 33–35).

FIGURE 31 Drawing by Lou Henry Hoover of pergola for garden. (Courtesy Stanford University Archives)

As for the cost of the construction, various figures have been given. In 1925 Lou said it was $170,000; four years later Birge Clark gave the amount as $150,000; in 1944 Herbert gave it as $137,000; and in his 1969 "Memoirs" Clark recalled it as $135,000.[88] In any case, the cost greatly exceeded the $50,000 Lou had contemplated with distress in her letter of 1917 complaining about Mullgardt's design. The discrepancy may have been due partly to the typical architect's tendency to give a client a low cost estimate at the beginning of a project, but it also no doubt reflects the typical clients' lack of awareness of what they actually need. As Birge Clark later said, the Hoovers originally wanted "a considerably smaller house than it turned out to be, but as often happens in architectural practice, an owner has various . . . needs, and just doesn't realize at first how much space their assembly is going to encompass."[89]

FIGURE 32 Hoover House from east, with garden pergola and pool. (*Sunset Magazine*, September 1928, 56)

Indeed, the size of the house became a sensitive point for the Hoovers, and they occasionally attempted to downplay or justify it. Sending a photograph to an acquaintance in 1933, Lou emphasized that it made the building look "so much larger than it really is."[90] And when the house was under construction, Herbert wrote, apparently in reaction to comments about the building's size, "my family is building a 'palace' containing seven rooms and a basement, a kitchen and a garage."[91] The "seven rooms" he had in mind must have been the living room, dining room, master bedroom, and Herbert's study, on the main

FIGURE 33 Hoover House nearing completion, 1920, garden façade. (Courtesy Herbert Hoover Presidential Library)

floor, and the two boys' rooms and Lou's study, on the upper floor. This ignores the large entrance hall, stair hall, "Library Alcove," and "Belgian Alcove," not to mention dressing rooms, servants' dining room, and so forth. And the lower floor, which Herbert dismissed as a "basement," had as many rooms as the other two floors combined. Using the designations on Birge Clark's floor plan of this lower level, these included six servant's rooms; two guest rooms and a guest sitting room; boys' playroom; cloak room; steno's room; children's nurse; visiting children's playroom; laundry; furnace room; and storeroom. Some of these spaces eventually had flexible uses: the boys' playroom, for example, was reportedly used as a press room when Hoover became a national figure accompanied by reporters.

Despite the seeming excess of the house, the Hoovers made good use of it, at least sometimes. When Lou and the two Hoover sons moved in, in 1920, they brought along several employees who had previously worked for the family in Palo Alto or Washington, including a valet, a cook, and a gardener and his family.[92]

FIGURE 34 Hoover House nearing completion, 1920, terrace off living room. (Courtesy Herbert Hoover Presidential Library)

FIGURE 35 Hoover House nearing completion, 1920, garden side. (Courtesy Herbert Hoover Presidential Library)

Lou continued to travel frequently to the East Coast to be with Herbert, who in early 1921 became secretary of commerce in the Harding administration. The teenaged Herbert Jr. and Allan remained in school in Palo Alto, so Lou engaged a graduate-student engineer, who was a family acquaintance, to oversee the household. And she invited two other Stanford students to live in the house. It therefore had as many as ten residents during this period, even when Lou and Herbert were not there. Moreover, there were people who worked in the house though not living there, such as two women who served as Lou's secretaries or assistants.[93] And at those times when Lou and Herbert did reside at the house, they typically had house guests—as when Lou, in July 1928, wrote of imminent plans for "sleeping and feeding people inside the pueblo walls."

Except for summer vacations, Herbert did not spend much time in the house. Lou was there more often, but even her visits were "all too infrequent," as Birge Clark put it.[94] Both Hoovers, however, considered this their real home, to which they returned as often as possible, and where they chose to reside on important occasions. They were there, for example, when Herbert accepted the Republican Party's nomination for president, in August 1928, and again when the election was held on November 7. When the news of Hoover's success was received at Stanford, a large group of students and others (including John Philip Sousa and his band) surged up to the house to cheer the president-elect and his family. A photograph of this event shows the Hoovers and many invited guests assembled on the roof terraces—perhaps the fullest use of these areas the house ever witnessed (Fig. 36).

FIGURE 36 Hoover House, the night of November 6, 1928, with the Hoovers and guests on the roof terraces. (Courtesy Hoover Institution Archives)

During Hoover's presidency, the family naturally spent little time in California. The house became an object of curiosity, which created security problems. In 1929 a newspaper reported:

> Souvenir hunters among the thousands of tourists and sightseers who journey to President Hoover's home in Palo Alto have made it necessary to establish private detectives around the grounds.
>
> Word came recently to the White House that collectors were taking, one by one, the flagstones which line the automobile drive to the President's front door.

FIGURE 37 Hoover House, dining room, before 1929. (Courtesy Hoover Institution Archives)

> Rose bushes and vines are being clipped, bits of stucco chiseled from the outside walls and pieces of the Spanish awnings torn off for mementoes. . . .
>
> [The house] is visited by thousands of tourists every month. The student body at Stanford has undertaken to protect the home as much as possible by reporting all instances of vandalism.[95]

After Hoover's term as president ended in early 1933, following his reelection defeat, the family was able to spend more time at its California home, although Herbert came to consider it too remote from the national centers of power and the activities in which he was involved, and he increasingly spent time on the East Coast.[96] In 1940 he decided to live principally in New York, and Lou followed

FIGURE 38 Hoover House, terrace off living room, facing northwest, probably 1920s. (Courtesy Hoover Institution Archives)

him, although they still returned to Stanford most summers and for important events such as the dedication of the Hoover Institution and when Lou gave the university's commencement address in 1941.[97]

Despite the relative infrequency of the Hoovers' residence in the house, Lou considered it the permanent family home. In a letter to the author Anna Hong Rutt, in 1933, she wrote as if the family had lived there continuously for a long time.[98] The following are some passages suggestive of the family's life there:

> The arrangement of the furniture is quite different now from when that picture was taken. [Lou enclosed photographs, which have not survived.] We are much given to moving things about, and nothing stays very long in the same place. . . .

FIGURE 39 Hoover House, terrace off living room, facing southeast, probably 1920s. (Courtesy Hoover Institution Archives)

When there is a small number in the family, we usually eat at a small table in the window [in the alcove at the end of the dining room, shown in Fig. 37], where we get the full beauty of mountains and valley with San Francisco bay running through it. When there are too many for that nook, we come on out into the main dining room. Many years ago I had made three tables, such as the one in the center of photograph D. . . . At the smaller table . . . any number from two to ten may be comfortable, or its duplicate can be alongside making one large table which will hold up to fourteen. . . . Or as often happens on really festive occasions (and remember we live on a campus and gatherings are frequent) we [create] a horseshoe or rectangular table. . . .

FIGURE 40 Hoover House, upper terrace, looking north, before 1929. (Courtesy Hoover Institution Archives)

The windows are all French windows, so that one may come and go from the terraces or walk outside perfectly simply. . . .

The furniture in the living room picture . . . is quite different now, as tables and sofas wander about according as it is brilliant warm sunshine outside and all attention is focused toward the windows, or if cold weather and rainy days are here, we turn to the fire. . . .

This terrace (photograph F) is where we live a great deal of the time,—for nine months of the year it is the family living room, and also has the very gorgeous views out across the valley to the mountains.

Evenings are nearly always cold here. And when the young people are dancing inside at night and come out, it is apt to be a bit chilly. [There is] a large fireplace that gives not only the effect of warmth, but real warmth for quite a radius. . . .

I have gone into all this detail that you might see how compact and simply arranged and yet adequate for a family of our size this plan is, and how perfectly naturally it fits together to get the best of the views and the sunshine appropriate for the use of each particular room. And then how simply the outside of the whole thing fits together when it is covered with plaster. . . .

The whole theme is that it is a very simple house, made to be lived in and on by the family that built it.

Chapter Three WHAT KIND OF ARCHITECTURE IS IT?

The architecture of the Lou Henry Hoover House has puzzled observers since the building's construction, and especially when Herbert Hoover's election to the presidency in 1928 focused attention on him and his family. In what style is the house? What are its sources or precedents? The answers have been amazingly diverse. In roughly the chronological order in which they were first proposed, they include: Pueblo Mexican Spanish;[1] Mediterranean or Italian;[2] Zuni;[3] Mission Pueblo;[4] Modernistic;[5] Oriental;[6] Early American Aztec;[7] Hispano-Moorish;[8] Algerian;[9] Hopi;[10] no historical style;[11] Mission Revival;[12] and International Style.[13]

Positions have been taken by journalists, historians, the general public, the professional architects involved in the project, and the Hoovers themselves. One would suppose that the statements by the Hoovers and their architects would be authoritative. But these remarks are themselves diverse and contradictory, those of Lou Henry Hoover not quite agreeing with those of her husband, nor with those of Arthur Clark or his son Birge. In fact, Birge Clark, who addressed the question more extensively than anyone else, gave various answers—some of them conflicting—at different times of his life.

The main cause of the confusion has no doubt been the unusual character of the house, which has frustrated observers' efforts to describe it in familiar terms. But the diversity of stylistic labels attached to the house has also reflected the attitudes and backgrounds of the individual labelers, as well as the time period of the labeling. The controversy over the building's style thus touches on larger issues about changing perceptions of architecture in the twentieth century.

Some designations that have been applied to the house can be dismissed easily. In July 1928 an editor of *Sunset Magazine*—one of many periodicals at that time anxious to publish articles about the home of the presidential candidate—wrote to Birge Clark and asked him to confirm that its style was "an adaptation of the Early American along Aztec lines."[14] Clark replied politely, "I am afraid this is not quite correct," and proposed a different answer.

The following month, a San Jose newspaper described the house as "Hispano-Moorish," a vague designation that might apply to a number of styles of architecture, none of them quite appropriate to the Hoover House.[15] In 1929 the magazine *Arts and Decoration* referred to the building's "Oriental inspiration" and "Oriental square form."[16] And the building has occasionally been called "Mission Revival," a term which in California usually refers to architecture inspired by the mission churches of the Spanish colonizers in the eighteenth and nineteenth centuries—structures that normally have sloping, tiled roofs, which are notably absent from the Hoover House.[17]

In recent decades the term "International Style" has often been applied to the house, even on an official plaque placed on the property in 1978.[18] The unadorned cubic nature of the house does invite comparison with the type of modern architecture dubbed International Style by Henry-Russell Hitchcock and Philip Johnson in 1932.[19] But the label is inappropriate in this case: first, because the Hoover House predates International-Style modernism, which developed in Europe in the 1920s; and, more to the point, because the house lacks several essential traits of the International Style. As defined by Hitchcock and Johnson, International-Style architecture had a "volumetric" quality, suggesting light-weight, nonbearing walls, and a structure of steel or reinforced-concrete columns. In contrast, the Hoover House has a massive appearance, suggesting thick bearing walls, despite the fact that its structure is a reinforced-concrete frame. And in contrast with the sharp, machine-like quality of International-Style buildings, the Hoover House has rounded corners and irregularities, for example in the wall above the fireplace on the main terrace (seen in Figs. 9 and 30). Moreover, International-Style surfaces were normally smooth and painted white, while the Hoover House originally was unpainted, exposing the rough surface and warm gray tones of the stucco plastered over the walls.

Reference to the International Style does, however, suggest comparison of the Hoover House to the avant-garde work of the architect Irving Gill in Southern California, of the 1910s—work whose cubic purity is sometimes seen as a precursor of the International Style in America.[20] Birge Clark reportedly denied that either he or Mrs. Hoover was aware of Gill's work.[21] But several articles on Gill had appeared in popular magazines before the Hoover House was designed. *Sunset Magazine*, for example, in 1915 had an piece on Gill's Banning House in Los Angeles, entitled "California's First Cubist House"; and *The Craftsman* in 1916 published an illustrated article written by Gill himself, "The Home of the Future" (Fig. 41).[22] The ideas Gill expressed in this article would no doubt have resonated with Lou Henry Hoover, especially statements such as, "We must dare to be simple . . . must break through convention and get down to fundamental

FIGURE 41 Irving Gill, drawing of Olmsted House, San Diego. (*The Craftsman*, May 1916, 140)

truths"; and he called for a "sanitary, labor-saving house, one where the maximum of comfort may be had with the minimum of drudgery."[23]

If Lou did know of Gill's work, it may have helped shape her attitudes about house design. But Gill's influence alone would not explain the distinctive character of the Hoover House. Gill's designs had greater precision of geometric form, with none of the idiosyncratic irregularities that distinguish the Hoover House. Moreover, the statements of the Hoovers themselves and their architects, regarding influences and sources, point in different directions from the stark modernism of Gill.

In 1921, as the house was being completed, Arthur Clark published a book on design principles, which included two photographs of the building and brief remarks about it (Figs. 42–43). Clark stated, "Prototypes for its style are found in part in the warm Mediterranean countries, and in part in the plain country houses found in Italy and the southwestern United States."[24]

Birge Clark was more specific, in his early statements on the subject. In July 1928, answering the *Sunset Magazine* editor who thought the house was Early American and Aztec, he wrote, "You might state that it shows marked Pueblo or Algerian influence."[25] But then he said, "Mrs. Hoover has always objected to having it called Pueblo, and I have always felt that it was the Algerian houses which gave her her original ideas."[26]

Despite this statement that Lou rejected the Pueblo connection, there is evidence that it had been in her mind from the beginning. The earliest known reference to the building's style, when it was still being designed in 1919, is in a letter written by Lou's private secretary and friend Dare Stark.[27] She wrote, "The lady is occupied these days correcting Mr. Clark's plans of the new house every time he draws them. It is going to be unique—Pueblo Mexican Spanish with flat roofs." It is unlikely that Dare Stark invented this designation herself; she must have based it on some kind of information from Lou.

FIGURE 42 Hoover House from north, at completion, 1920. (Arthur B. Clark, *Art Principles in House, Furniture, and Village Building* [Stanford, CA, 1921], 47)

FIGURE 43 Hoover House, upper level on garden side, at completion, 1920. (Arthur B. Clark, *Art Principles* [Stanford, CA, 1921], 47)

But Birge Clark became increasingly adamant that there was no Pueblo influence at all, a position that may reflect the low esteem many professional architects of the time had for the Pueblo Revival. He may also have become annoyed by journalists' attraction to exotic-sounding labels like Aztec, Pueblo, Hopi, and Zuni. (An article in the *Cleveland Plain Dealer* in 1928 had described the house as "the Zuni Pueblo Style.")[28] Clark did, however, admit an "Algerian" influence—at least for a while. Following his exchange with the *Sunset Magazine* editor, he answered other inquiries similarly, which led to the identification of the style of the house as Algerian in several articles of the period, including one in a German women's magazine.[29] In September 1928, for example, Birge wrote to a journalist:

> Mrs. Hoover desired a house which should have all the roof spaces available for use, and also a house which should look more or less like blocks piled up. It has always been our opinion [that is, his and his father's] that the Algerian houses which Mrs. Hoover had seen inspired this motif. It was specifically not the pueblo, altho the finished house somewhat resembles this type of architecture.[30]

Shortly thereafter, another magazine editor wrote to Birge, assuming—as did so many people—that the house was Pueblo in style: "We want, through this article, to familiarize our readers with the Hopi Indian style of architecture."[31] Birge replied:

> This architecture is not Hopi Indian, altho it does bear a resemblance, no doubt, to the pueblos found in the southwestern part of the United States. I would rather say that it is reminiscent of the flat-roofed Algerian buildings, altho it was designed without any conscious historical style, but rather to produce a house in which all of the roof areas could be used as living terraces.[32]

One detects here a shift in Birge's thinking. Although he previously had stated that Algerian architecture had "inspired" Mrs. Hoover and "gave her her original ideas," he now maintained that the house was only "reminiscent" of Algerian architecture. This revision was to accelerate in succeeding years. In his 1969 memoirs, Birge wrote that "the Hoovers did not want the house to be related to any historical style," and "it has frequently been called Algerian or Pueblo Indian in style. This is purely coincidental."[33]

Clark later made a little joke about this. When asked about the style of the house in an interview in 1978, he answered, "Some people called it Hopi, some called it Algerian. I guess that's why it was finally called International."[34]

This position, that the house was essentially without style or historical influence, may result from a modernist view, common from the 1920s on, that since form should strictly follow function, "style" is superfluous and to be avoided. It is unlikely that either Arthur or Birge Clark personally subscribed to this notion,

FIGURE 44 Taos Pueblo, New Mexico. (Author)

given the nature of their own architectural designs, but Birge may have come to think that the Hoover House did represent this kind of pure functionalism or stylelessness. It is doubtful, however, that any architectural design can be devoid of style or influence from the past, even if the designer attempts it. And Lou's own statements reveal that while she was not trying to create a house of one specific style, she was nevertheless inspired by architecture she had seen in her travels.

In fact, the designations Algerian—or more generally North African—and Pueblo may both be applied with some validity to the Hoover House. Both represent a type of building found in several parts of the world with relatively warm, dry climates, in which flat-roofed structures made of stone or adobe brick, often given a smooth plaster surface, are appropriate to the climate and the available building materials (Figs. 44–45). The Hoover House is similar to such architecture not only in its cubic forms and unadorned surfaces, but in the rounded edges and irregular shapes of many of its parts, suggestive of the imprecise, handworked nature of adobe construction. And the original color of the stucco surface—darker, warmer in tone, and rougher in texture than the house as it presently is painted—would have been more suggestive of adobe architecture than is the case today.

A connection with Pueblo architecture is suggested also by a puzzling detail of the house: the group of potentially dangerous "steps" at the roofline of the entrance façade, to the left of the front door (Figs. 46–47). This feature was noted

FIGURE 45 Market in Biskra, Algeria. (*The National Geographic Magazine*, August 1908, 583)

later by Birge Clark as one of the few parts of the house that had "no functional purpose and were strictly aesthetic."[35] Precedents in European architecture would be difficult or impossible to find. But such steps, at the edge of a roof and precariously positioned or reached only by a removable ladder, are found in indigenous flat-roofed architecture from various parts of the world, especially in the Pueblo villages of New Mexico and Arizona (Fig. 48).

The Hoovers themselves, with their strong desire to keep their personal lives private, made almost no public statements about their house. Only toward the end of his life did Herbert speak of the house for publication. In his memoirs he wrote:

> Mrs. Hoover had long dreamed of building a house upon a near-by campus hill where the glorious views of the mountains and bay came into sight. It was to be a Hopi house (not Spanish) with flat roofs, and all modern inside. She had leased the lot some years before, and, upon our return to California, she resurrected her preliminary architectural drawings and began to build. The house was all her own making, but the dreams which she built into it had a rude awakening. I again had to be away at intervals over many years and she, in loyalty and service, had to make more new and temporary homes. The house, however, reflected well her excellent sense of taste and form in arrangement and workmanship. It was her own blend of fine living and the new spirit of native western architecture to modern America. With outdoor living, its terraces, its

FIGURE 46 Hoover House, detail of entrance façade showing "steps" at edge of roof. (Author)

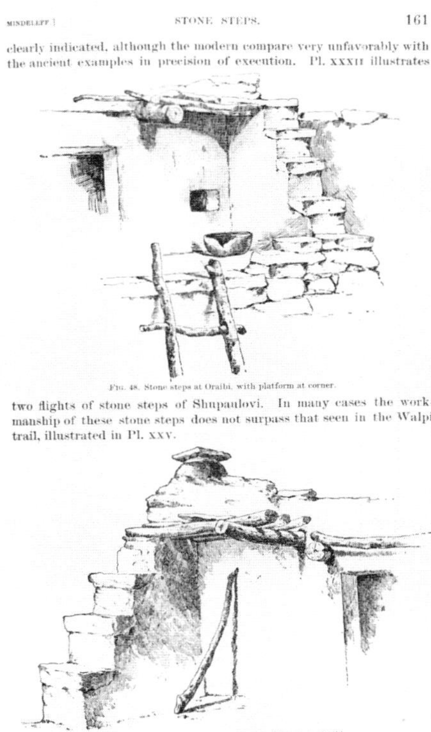

MINDELEFF] STONE STEPS. 161

clearly indicated, although the modern compare very unfavorably with the ancient examples in precision of execution. Pl. XXXII illustrates

Fig. 48. Stone steps at Oraibi, with platform at corner.

two flights of stone steps of Shupaulovi. In many cases the workmanship of these stone steps does not surpass that seen in the Walpi trail, illustrated in Pl. XXV.

Fig. 49. Stone steps, with platform at chimney, in Oraibi.

8 ETH——11

FIGURE 47 Hoover House, roof terrace with "steps" at edge of roof. (Author)

FIGURE 48 Drawings of roof steps, Hopi pueblo of Oraibi, Arizona. (Victor Mindeleff, "A Study of Pueblo Architecture," in *U.S. Bureau of American Ethnology, Eighth Annual Report* [Washington DC, 1891], 161)

> foreground of the University, its magnificent views of the mountains and bay, it was an expression of herself. The house was two years in the building and was not completed when we migrated for another thirteen-year period—except to return sometimes for a few days in the summer.[36]

As for Lou's recorded comments about the house, they paint a more complex picture than Herbert's categorical "Hopi" designation. She did at least once use the word "Pueblo" to describe the house. In her previously quoted letter to a friend, in 1928, she spoke of her frequent and often unplanned entertaining of guests and added, "So I have no idea what the demands will be for sleeping and feeding people inside the pueblo walls."[37] This seems to have a light-hearted, almost jocular tone, but it suggests that Lou was familiar with the common perception of the house as Pueblo in style and was not offended by it.

The only substantial record of Lou's thoughts about the house and its style is found in a letter she wrote in 1933 in response to an inquiry from Anna Hong Rutt, an art teacher who was writing a book on "home planning."[38] In her letter, Rutt mentioned that she had known Lou's mother many years earlier in Monterey, California; Lou responded warmly to this connection, which no doubt made her more willing to speak candidly about the house. After explaining to Rutt that she disliked publicity and did not normally answer inquiries, she wrote,

> However, I have such an interest in architecture myself and in the development of simple living quarters, that I am only too glad to help.

FIGURE 49 Stanford University Quad, designed by Frederick Law Olmsted and Charles Coolidge about 1890, view of part of Inner Quad. (Courtesy Stanford University Archives)

> I very largely planned the house myself with a most considerate architect who humored me whenever I wanted to get away from Beaux-Arts conditions! We did not make any attempt to have the house of any style or period. I wanted to make it just as simple in line and surface as could be done. You will find no feature of it for purely ornamental purposes.
>
> I have liked the primitive houses in many lands especially for their simplicity. And my husband and I had said we wanted this house to be a collection of rooms where we wanted them for living purposes enclosed by plain wall surfaces. . . . We felt that it [should be] in decided harmony with the architecture of the University on whose campus it sits [Fig. 49]. The University is of an American developed Spanish style that shows distinctly Moorish characteristics. This house, while very much earlier in feeling, nevertheless does not combat what might have been a later development from its own time.[39]

It is unclear what Lou meant by "Moorish," in the penultimate sentence; the word had a variety of meanings at that time.[40] As for the puzzling last sentence Lou perhaps meant that the house was more primitive in feeling than the architecture of the Stanford Quad but could be seen as representing an earlier stage in some historical development that led to the Quad.

Lou then described the siting of the house, its views, and its organization, saying, "We think that in our climate much more use should be made of the roofs of the houses than had been done up to the time we built it. We are able to sit

FIGURE 50 Hoover House, roof terraces atop main floor. (Courtesy Hoover Institution Archives)

out on any part of the house [Lou's emphasis]. And there are steps leading from one elevation to another." She then described the color of the house and addressed the question of its "Pueblo" character:

> The outside of the house is plastered a soft cream color. And if we had been trying to make a pueblo period house, as has often been said, the inside would have been completely plastered. However, we were building the house that pleased us in detail, not one attempting to conform to any pattern.

Lou went on to describe the interior of the house, the fondness she and her husband had for "panelled walls," the eclectic variety of furnishings from many of the countries in which they had lived, and the family's frequent use of the terraces.

In contrast to Herbert's straightforward identification of the house as "Hopi," Lou reveals here a more complex view. The design was shaped mainly by considerations of function and aesthetic preference, not historical styles. Nevertheless, she had been inspired by things she had seen, especially in the architecture of "primitive houses in many lands." It was not a "pueblo period house," but mainly because the interior was not plastered in a Pueblo manner. In effect she was acknowledging that the exterior could be considered Pueblo in character.

For both the Hoovers the house had some relationship with Pueblo Indian architecture. The connection was less clear-cut for Lou than for Herbert, as she had been inspired by many kinds of "primitive" buildings. It is relevant, therefore, to inquire into the types of non-European architecture—Native American and others—with which the Hoovers were familiar.

Chapter Four THE HOOVERS AND INDIGENOUS ARCHITECTURE

Lou Henry's childhood papers, preserved at the Herbert Hoover Presidential Library in West Branch, Iowa, reveal that she had an interest in Native Americans from an early age.[1] Born in 1874 in Waterloo, Iowa (not far from Herbert Hoover's birthplace, although the two of them did not meet until they were students at Stanford), Lou as a child moved frequently with her family: to Texas in 1879; back to Iowa in 1880; to Kansas briefly in 1887; to Whittier, California, later that year; and finally to Monterey, California, in 1890.[2]

Among Lou's school papers are brief essays on "Mound Builders" and "Indians," written in 1886 when she was eleven years old, and more substantial essays, undated but probably written when she was in high school in Whittier, on "The Missions of California" and "Acoma."[3] Her notes on Acoma, perhaps a draft for a paper, describe in some detail this mesa-top pueblo in New Mexico (Fig. 51), focusing on its "curious houses . . . built of gray adobe in a terrace of three successive stories, standing in three parallel rows, each a thousand feet long, and divided within into cozy little tenements." Her language indicates that the description comes at least partly from visual images, not just written sources, and it suggests careful observation.

It is possible that the Henry family had learned of Acoma and other Pueblo villages—perhaps even visited them—during their trip on the Santa Fe Railway when they moved to Southern California in 1887.[4] In any case, accounts of Southwest Indian life and architecture were beginning to appear in the 1880s, in ethnographic and archaeological studies such as those of Lewis Morgan and Victor Mindeleff, and in more popular forms, such as a series of articles by Frank Cushing in *The Century Magazine* in 1882 and 1883, illustrated with many images of Zuni Pueblo in New Mexico (Fig. 52).[5]

The young Lou Henry was fascinated by the simple architectural forms of adobe construction, whether in Indian pueblos or in the early buildings of Spanish California. In a diary entry of December 1889, she described the adobe Pico House, near Whittier, to which she had traveled by horseback with friends; she

FIGURE 51 Acoma Pueblo, New Mexico, photograph included by David Starr Jordan in his autobiography. (*The Days of a Man* [New York, 1922], opposite p. 632)

even drew a little plan of the building between her lines of writing.[6] When her family moved to Monterey the next year, she described the old Spanish town as "all adobes and crooked streets and funny places. I think I will like it very much."[7] Drawings in Lou's sketch books of this period reveal her attraction to this type of construction, with its geometric forms and picturesque details (Figs. 53–54).[8]

Herbert Hoover, too, was interested in Native Americans from an early age. Following the death of his father in 1880, he lived for a while with an aunt and an uncle who was the government agent for the Osage and Kew nations in Indian Territory (Oklahoma); he later recalled with affection his association with Indian schoolmates, from whom he had "learned much aboriginal lore of the woods and streams."[9] In 1923, Lou mentioned in a letter to a friend, "My husband has always been interested in Indian affairs, from the time he was a very small boy and spent months at a time with his uncle on one of the largest reservations. His life in the Southwest naturally often took him amongst the different tribes."[10] "His life in the Southwest" probably refers to Herbert's work as surveyor and geologist in several Western states following his graduation from Stanford, including work in the Steeple Rock area of southwestern New Mexico.[11]

During the period when Herbert and Lou were students at Stanford, public interest in American Indians, especially the Pueblo peoples, became widespread. The adventurer and journalist Charles Lummis helped popularize Indian culture with his writings, and among Lummis's friends were the president of Stanford University, David Starr Jordan, and his wife, Jessie Knight Jordan. In the summer of 1898 the Jordans took a trip with Lummis to the Grand Canyon and to Acoma Pueblo in New Mexico, an expedition documented by photographs taken

FIGURE 52 Drawing of dance in Zuni Pueblo, New Mexico. (Frank Cushing, "My Adventures in Zuñi," pt. 1, *The Century Illustrated Monthly Magazine*, December 1882, 205)

by Mrs. Jordan—perhaps including several that were later reproduced in President Jordan's autobiography (see Fig. 51).[12] It is not known to what extent Herbert Hoover and Lou Henry, as students, shared the interest in things Indian shown by others at Stanford. But they must have been exposed to the increasing publicity about the subject in the popular press.

On the day after their marriage, in 1899, Lou and Herbert took a ship bound for China, where he had been put in charge of managing the mines of the British

FIGURE 53 Sketches by Lou Henry of details of "California Missions," c. 1890. (Courtesy Herbert Hoover Presidential Library)

firm of Bewick and Moreing. This began a long period of living in far-flung locations in Asia and elsewhere and of traveling frequently around the world as they moved from one assignment to another, traveled back and forth to Herbert's headquarters in London, and made periodic returns to the United States. Lou's correspondence, diaries, and the scrapbooks she assembled during this time reveal her intense interest in the geography, life, architecture, and culture of all the places where she lived and traveled, including parts of China, Japan, Australia, Burma, New Zealand, Samoa, Ceylon, South Africa, and the countries surrounding the Mediterranean Sea.[13]

Shortly after establishing a home in Tientsin, China, in 1899, Lou wrote of her explorations of this city, with its "tiny tortuous lanes winding thro' a most interesting maze of brick and mud buildings."[14] The Hoovers' status as well-to-do

FIGURE 54 Sketch by Lou Henry of stairway at San Gabriel Mission, California, c. 1890. (Courtesy Herbert Hoover Presidential Library)

foreign professionals required their living in relatively affluent conditions, and their own houses were usually of Western style (Fig. 55).[15] It is notable, however, that Lou's observations about the places she visited tended to minimize upper-class or grand architecture, sometimes calling it "pretentious," and reveal more interest in simple, native dwellings.[16]

During these years of traveling and living abroad, especially from 1899 to about 1910, Lou filled numerous scrapbooks with mementos—especially photographs, many taken by herself, of her family, landscapes, local people, and architecture.[17] There are many photographs of traditional, native buildings in such places as China, Burma, New Guinea, Fiji, Samoa, New Zealand, Hawaii, South Africa, Ceylon, and Egypt (Figs. 56–57). In light of Birge Clark's statement that Lou had been inspired by "Algerian houses [she] had seen," one wonders especially about her familiarity with North Africa. Unfortunately, there is no known evidence of her visiting Algeria, although it is very likely she did, during the ship voyages that passed through the Suez Canal and the Mediterranean on the way to England. Clark may have been using the word "Algerian" to mean North African in general, and it is known that Lou did visit Egypt, especially those parts adjacent to the Suez Canal—where she collected photographs of vernacular Egyptian architecture that suggest comparison with the house she later built at Stanford (Fig. 57).

FIGURE 55 The Hoovers' house in Tientsin, China, c. 1900. (Courtesy Hoover Institution Archives)

Lou and Herbert also returned frequently to the United States, together or separately, and many of these trips required traveling across the country, taking trains either on the northern route, or on the southern route by the Santa Fe Railway.[18] During this period, the Santa Fe capitalized on Americans' burgeoning interest in Southwest Indian culture, with promotional literature and the Harvey House hotels, restaurants, and shops, in which Indian crafts were exhibited and sold, and whose architecture simulated Pueblo and Spanish mission construction.[19] One of the architects of these Santa Fe Railway and Harvey Company structures was Charles Whittlesey, who later designed—for the Hoovers—the first student-union buildings at Stanford (see Fig. 64).

On one of her cross-country trips, in January 1904, Lou made notes on a Santa Fe Railway map, marking the family's progress by train through Arizona and New Mexico.[20] She was apparently continuing her study of Native American culture at this time. Among the items in her collected papers are several illustrations of Zuni Pueblo, taken from the 1904 annual report of the Bureau of American Ethnology (Fig. 58).[21] The lavishly produced and illustrated annual reports of this government bureau were devoted largely to Native American history and culture and constituted the most substantial and scholarly literature on the subject during this period. If Lou had access to these volumes, besides the one of 1904, she would have had the most up-to-date information on the archaeology and architecture of the Pueblo Indians.

FIGURE 56 Buildings in Pago Pago, Samoa, photographs taken by Lou Henry Hoover, July 12, 1905. (Courtesy Herbert Hoover Presidential Library)

FIGURE 57 Buildings in Egypt, photograph acquired by Lou Henry Hoover in 1905. (Courtesy Herbert Hoover Presidential Library)

On a more popular level, *The National Geographic Magazine* at this time was probably the most significant vehicle for articles on, and illustrations of, Native American and other non-European cultures throughout the world. In about 1902, Lou became one of the first members of the National Geographic Society, and she no doubt received its magazine regularly.[22] The publication during this period contained articles on the American Southwest and its pueblos, as well as on indigenous peoples of North Africa and other parts of the world (see Fig. 45). Typical was an article in 1911 on the "Snake Dance of the Hopi," illustrated with photographs of buildings in the Hopi pueblos of Walpi and Oraibi (Fig. 59).[23]

Another source of information about Native Americans, for the Hoovers, was Mary Austin, prolific author of popular books on the American West. Lou and Herbert met Austin in about 1910 in London and developed a close friendship with her during the following decade; their correspondence dealt with a variety of progressive issues in the arts and society.[24] Many of the letters between Austin and Lou Henry Hoover in the late 1910s concerned their mutual interest in Pueblo Indian crafts. Austin, who was living in Santa Fe at the time, sent Lou information on Pueblo pottery and arranged purchases of it, as Lou became an enthusiastic collector of Indian rugs and pottery.[25] A letter she wrote to Austin,

FIGURE 58 Part of Zuni Pueblo, New Mexico, illustration saved by Lou Henry Hoover, from *Twenty-Third Annual Report of the Bureau of American Ethnology* (Washington DC, 1904), plate CX. (Courtesy Herbert Hoover Presidential Library)

FIGURE 59 Hopi pueblo of Walpi, Arizona. ("The Snake Dance," *The National Geographic Magazine*, February 1911, 109)

undated but evidently from the mid-1910s, acknowledges receipt of a shipment of pots and suggests that Lou's interest in Indian wares was influencing her ideas about house planning:

> The box of jars arrived. . . . They came in perfect condition—three Santo Domingo, one Zuni, one Tewa, and the San Ildefonso water jar . . . now they are all over the living room. . . . And the shining black water jar is quite the loveliest thing I could imagine! It sets me to planning all sorts of appropriate backgrounds for it—I shall have to have an Indian room some day—or perhaps better an Indian porch. . . . I am keeping your letter, and as soon as I have a more concrete idea of how many jars my California house can hold, and what kind, I shall let you know.[26]

Since this letter is undated, it is unclear which house Lou was installing these pots in. But she was collecting them for the "California house" she was planning, and she was envisioning an Indian room or porch for them. Early photographs of the main terrace of the Hoover House show Indian rugs prominently placed on it, suggesting that Lou may have considered this her Indian porch (see Fig. 38). According to a story in a San Jose newspaper in 1928, the house contained "Mexican pottery . . . and Indian rugs."[27] Lou used Indian pottery and rugs also in the cabins at Rapidan Camp, the retreat in Virginia she created following Herbert's assumption of the presidency in 1929 (Fig. 60).[28]

In late 1922 the Hoovers visited the governor of New Mexico in Santa Fe.[29] Lou became interested in contemporary works of art she saw there, and in subsequent correspondence with staff of the Museum of New Mexico she purchased

FIGURE 60 Interior of President's Cabin, Rapidan Camp, Virginia, with Indian rugs and pottery, c. 1931. (Courtesy Herbert Hoover Presidential Library)

several paintings of Indian subjects, including "Adobe Houses" by Carlos Vierra, a view of a pueblo by a "Mr. Rollins," and "two Taos pictures."[30] Herbert, who apparently remained in New Mexico after Lou's departure, was also involved in the negotiations about these works; a letter to Lou from the museum's librarian reported, "Am afraid that Mr. Hoover was not very enthusiastic about Mr. Rollins' picture of Zuni so I hesitated to send it. He seemed to like the . . . misty early morning picture of Jemez [another pueblo] that you liked, too."[31] Lou was furnishing the recently constructed Stanford house at this time, and despite the fact that the interiors were different in style from the exterior, she evidently wanted the interior decorations to accord, to some degree, with the Pueblo character of its external architecture.

In the late summer of 1941, Lou and Herbert and some friends took a leisurely automobile trip in southern Colorado and northern New Mexico. In a letter to a relative, describing the vacation, Lou's account of their travel through Pueblo country reveals their familiarity with the area:

> In the afternoon we had a fascinating mountain drive to Albuquerque (deliberately missing Santa Fe which we all knew well). And the road from Albuquerque to Gallup was even more interesting, via Laguna [Pueblo], looking off to the

FIGURE 61 Santa Fe Railway pavilion, Panama-Pacific Exposition, San Francisco, 1914. (*Sunset Magazine*, October 1914, 737)

highly colored mountains. . . . We got off to a late start in the morning, but we had another gorgeous mountain drive before us, through Winslow, Flagstaff, and Painted Desert. All along the way we saw Pueblo and Navajo settlements and sales stalls—and getting a glimpse of Acoma, miles in the distance. And always sunflowers! We had a good lunch at a Harvey House in Winslow.[32]

The Hoover House must also be seen within the context of the Pueblo Revival or "Puebloesque" style of architecture of the early twentieth century. Starting about 1900, Americans' fascination with things Indian led to the use of Pueblo forms in contemporary architecture, especially in the West and Southwest.[33] On one level this was just another of the numerous revival styles that had proliferated over the previous century—first Greek and Gothic, then Egyptian, Turkish, Chinese, and other exotic styles. The Pueblo Revival was different, however, in that it reflected, at least in the American Southwest, a regionalist concern for creating forms appropriate to the climate, topography, and culture of this part of the country.

At first this mode was used for buildings perceived as having some relevance, or at least proximity, to the pueblos, such as the structures for the Harvey Company and the Santa Fe Railway. The Pueblo Revival was used also for buildings at expositions, such as the New Mexico Building at the San Diego fair of 1915, where there was also a remarkable replica of the pueblo at Taos. There was a more modest Pueblo-style pavilion at the San Francisco fair of the same year (Fig. 61).

FIGURE 62 Bailey House ("Hopi House"), La Jolla, California, designed by Mead and Requa, architects, 1914. (*Western Architect*, June 29, 1920)

By this time, the Pueblo style was being used for a wider range of building types, including domestic architecture. A house erected at La Jolla in 1915 (published the following year in *The Craftsman*), by the architect Frank Mead, was a relatively authentic simulation of a Pueblo dwelling and was specifically called a "Hopi house" (Fig. 62).[34] Most such buildings were much less faithful than this, but they were still recognized as "Pueblo" by the general public, as the style came to be rather common in the American Southwest. This is no doubt why so many people assumed the Hoover House was Pueblo in style in the years following its construction, even though this was denied by Birge Clark.

By 1910, Pueblo-Revival buildings were being erected even in the San Francisco Bay Area, despite its topographic and climatic dissimilarity to the Pueblo lands of New Mexico and Arizona. This Bay Area phenomenon was stimulated in part by the presence of Charles Whittlesey, architect for the Santa Fe Railway and Harvey Company, who had come to San Francisco following the 1906 earthquake and designed several houses in the Pueblo style in San Francisco, such as the Ward House in 1912 (Fig. 63).[35] About 1913, Whittlesey was chosen as architect for the first student union at Stanford, consisting of the Men's Clubhouse and Women's Clubhouse, now parts of the Old Union complex (Fig. 64). Since this project had been initiated and largely financed by Herbert Hoover, it is likely that he played a role in hiring Whittlesey. Hoover reportedly wanted these clubhouses to be similar to buildings he had seen along the Santa Fe Railway.[36]

FIGURE 63 Ward House, San Francisco, built 1912, Charles Whittlesey, architect. (*Architect and Engineer*, May 1912, 84)

A much more modest house of this type, near Burlingame on the San Francisco Peninsula, was illustrated by Arthur Clark and identified as "Pueblo" in the book he published in 1921 (Fig. 65), in which he also illustrated the newly completed Hoover House. The Pueblo style came to be used especially for small, inexpensive buildings such as this because its simple massing and lack of ornament were economical. The resulting association of the Pueblo Revival with cheap construction was probably one of the reasons the style was often denigrated by respectable members of the architectural profession. This perception was recognized by a writer on architecture in 1928, who described Pueblo Indian buildings

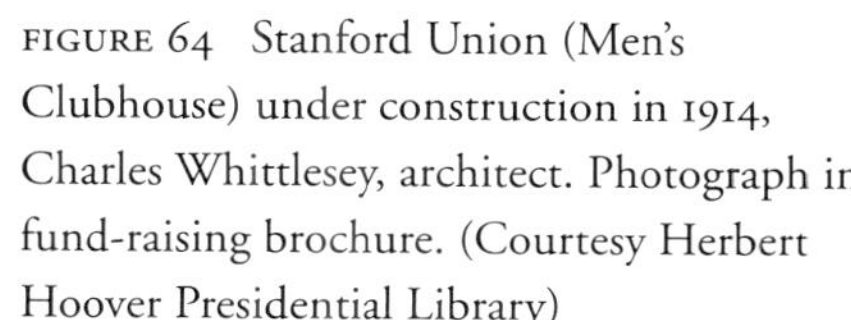

FIGURE 64 Stanford Union (Men's Clubhouse) under construction in 1914, Charles Whittlesey, architect. Photograph in fund-raising brochure. (Courtesy Herbert Hoover Presidential Library)

FIGURE 65 "A residence in 'Pueblo' style, at Easton, near Burlingame, Cal." (Arthur B. Clark, *Art Principles* [Stanford, CA, 1921], 21)

as "rudely constructed," and said, "One would think the average architect would recoil from the idea of being inspired in any way by such an untutored and barbaric performance"—although he did praise the simplicity and "harmony" of Pueblo architecture.[37]

The disdain of Puebloesque buildings in much of the architectural community no doubt contributed to Birge Clark's adamant stance that the Hoover House had not been inspired by the pueblos, and that the similarities were merely "coincidental."

It is true, however, that the Hoover House is different in character, and in motivation, from most examples of Pueblo-Revival architecture of the period. These differences make the Hoover House especially significant within the context of early twentieth-century architecture.

Chapter Five THE PRIMITIVE AND THE MODERN

Herbert Hoover's description of the house his wife built as "a Hopi house . . . and all modern inside" was an oversimplification, since "Hopi" does not fully explain the exterior, and the interior was not exactly "modern" in the usual sense of the word. Nevertheless, the concepts of the primitive and the modern are both relevant to the house, and their combination gave the building much of its distinctive character. Not unique in this regard, the Hoover House is one example of the interplay of primitive traditions and modern ideals in early twentieth-century architecture.

Herbert and Lou Henry Hoover were exemplars of a particular type of modernism and were publicly perceived as such, especially in the 1910s and 1920s. Trained in science and engineering, they were inclined to approach problems in a rational, no-nonsense way. This was often emphasized in the newspaper and magazine articles about them starting at the time of the First World War, and Herbert was commonly called "the Great Engineer."

This rational attitude shaped the Hoovers' architectural preferences. Herbert's main requirement for their house, according to Birge Clark, was that it be fireproof, and he wanted flat roofs so they could be made "useful." Lou, in describing the building to Anna Hong Rutt, wrote, "My husband and I had said we wanted this house to be a collection of rooms where we wanted them for living purposes, enclosed by plain wall surfaces," and "you will find no feature of it for purely ornamental purposes."[1] For the Hoovers, simple, unadorned forms were clearly associated with functionalism and practicality.

Another modern trait found in the Hoovers—especially in Lou—was a belief in the virtue of vigorous exercise and healthy outdoor living, for both sexes. Since her childhood, Lou had participated in sports and other activities normally reserved for men, or had done them with unusual vigor (riding her horse "like a centaur"), and she became a strong proponent of the health benefits of outdoor life—the main cause she advocated in her long involvement in the Girl Scouts organization. In this regard she exemplified (in her dignified way, of course) the cult of physical health for women as well as men, which in the early twentieth century encouraged revolutions in traditional gender roles, in clothing, and in the design of houses and outdoor spaces.

One aspect of this movement can be seen in an article in *The Craftsman* in 1913, entitled "Open-Air Rooms and Sleeping Porches: The Revolt Against the Shut-in Houses of Our Forefathers." It extolled the benefits of sun and fresh air and called for the modern home to be "thrown open to the sunshine" and provide "verandas" and other outdoor spaces for use both during the day and at night.[2]

The architecture of Native Americans and other "primitive" peoples became associated with many of these modern ideals, and the pueblos of the American Southwest were especially appealing for their simplicity and apparent functionalism. More generally, the virtue of outdoor living became associated with Native Americans in the minds of many health cultists. This is seen, for example, in a book published in 1908, *What the White Race May Learn from the Indian.*[3] Its author, George Wharton James, focused on physical and mental health, with chapters extolling Native American superiority in regard to breathing, sleeping, walking and riding, diet, child rearing, nudity, and "the sex question." There are only a few references in the book to architecture, but all of them are to Pueblo buildings, and the book's frontispiece illustrates Hopis on the steps of one of the Pueblo structures at Mashonganavi. A chapter on outdoor sleeping has an illustration of "Terraced Houses of the Hopis, Allowing Sleeping Out of Doors."

The Hoover House terraces were reportedly used by the family for sleeping. One of the later occupants of the house, Jean Mosher Pitzer (wife of President Kenneth Pitzer) recalled that Lou "liked to sleep outdoors during the summer" and that she and the boys "would move the beds out . . . and there was one outside the president's bedroom."[4] Lou herself spoke about the use of the terraces, saying, "We are able to sit out on any part of the house [Lou's emphasis]," and stating that the main terrace, on the garden side of the house, "is where we live a great deal of the time—for nine months of the year it is the family living room." From this terrace, Lou continued, "stairs go up to the rest of the roofs, where one can wander all about from sun to shade according as the temperature of the day dictates."[5]

Since Pueblo-Revival architecture was relatively popular in the Western United States by the time the Hoover House was designed, the house was often identified by observers as belonging to this style. The motives of the Hoovers, however, were quite different from those of most of the builders of Puebloesque structures—commercial motives; promotion of Southwest culture in exposition and government buildings; regionalist pride; and fascination with the exoticism of things Indian.

The Hoovers, or at least Lou (as we know less about Herbert's views in this area), shared none of these motives. Lou had no desire to participate in exoticism or regional boosterism, which would surely have been repugnant to her. She was attracted to Pueblo and other primitive forms of architecture for the inherent virtues she found in them: simplicity, functionalism, close connection with nature, and the facilitation of healthy living.

This kind of appreciation of indigenous architecture, while not yet common in the early twentieth century, can be found in some professionals of the period. These were mostly avant-garde architects, and the qualities they admired in primitive traditions were those most compatible with the emerging modernist ideals. An article on Pueblo architecture in a 1906 issue of *The Architectural Record* proclaimed:

> If it be true . . . that the characteristics of good architecture are that a building shall be in harmony with its surroundings; that the exterior shall be in right relation to the interior, the elevation being a natural development of the plan; and that it shall be free from meaningless and meretricious ornament, then Pueblo American architecture is good architecture, and deserves a moment of consideration; and it further possesses the merit of being a frank and logical expression of its purpose, and of the materials used.[6]

Some of the most prominent modernist architects were attracted to Pueblo or other Native American architecture in this way. The Austrian émigré Rudolph Schindler visited Taos Pueblo in 1915, and it inspired him to design a "Country Home in Adobe Construction," which he nevertheless described as being forthrightly "of the twentieth century" (Fig. 66).[7] At about the same time, Frank Lloyd Wright became interested in Mesoamerican architecture, whose massive walls and geometric ornament influenced houses he subsequently built in the Los Angeles area (Fig. 67).[8] For Wright, these works had little to do with exoticism; he was simply using forms he considered expressive of his principles and appropriate to a regional modernism.

The Southern California work of Irving Gill, of the 1910s and 1920s, provides another example of the contribution of primitive forms to a fully modernist architecture. Gill's radically plain and cubic work (Fig. 68, and see Fig. 41) is recognized as having been inspired in part by his interest in North African and Native American Pueblo architecture—an interest reinforced by his association with Frank Mead, a passionate proponent of Native American rights, who designed the "Hopi House" at La Jolla (see Fig. 62).[9] But in contrast to Mead's literalism, Gill focused on the creation of an uncompromising modernism.

The constructive relationship between the primitive and the modern was found not only in America. In Europe at this time, some avant-garde modernists

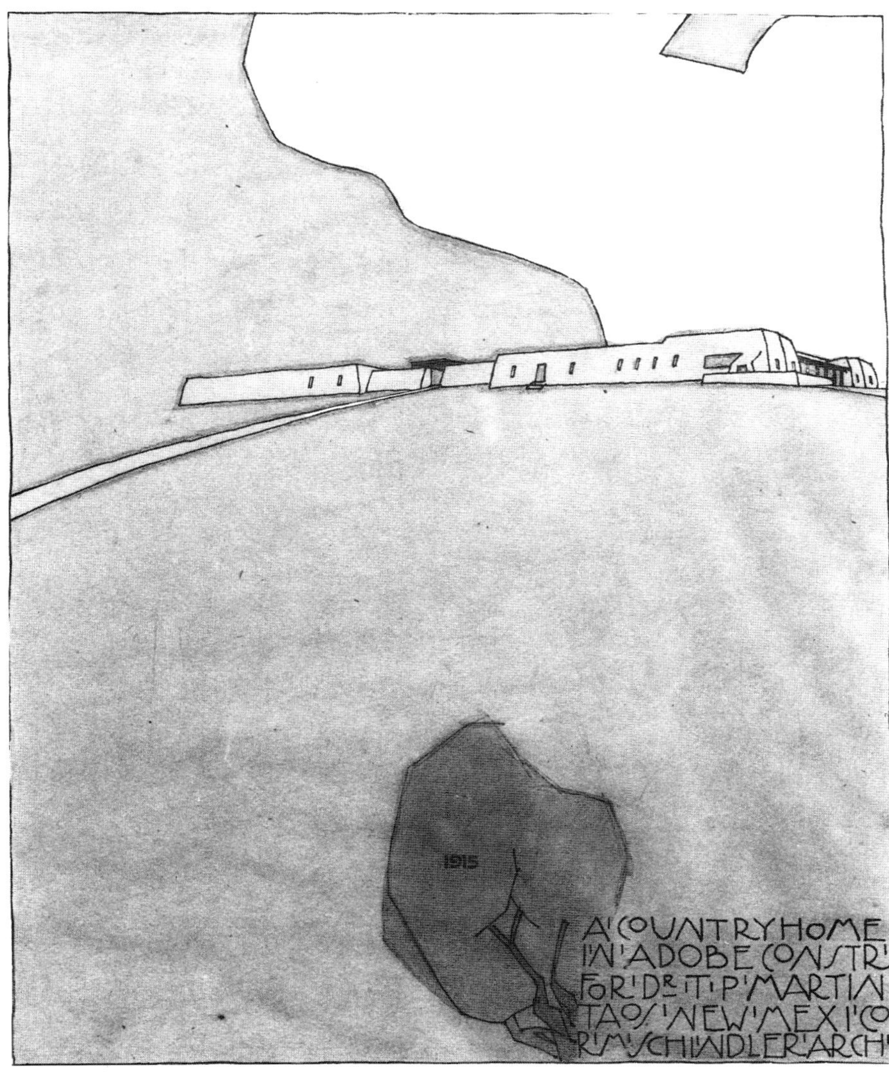

FIGURE 66 Rudolph Schindler, drawing of Martin House project, Taos, New Mexico, 1915. (Courtesy Architecture and Design Collection, University Art Museum, University of California, Santa Barbara)

were also inspired by non-Western building types. Le Corbusier, for example, was greatly impressed with North African and Middle Eastern architecture, in which he found qualities of simplicity and geometric purity that were central to the modernism he helped create in the 1920s.[10]

The Hoover House is therefore just one example of a phenomenon in modern architecture: an interest in primitive forms and building types, not for their exotic or eclectic appeal, but for inherent traits that the pioneers of modernism found useful in their formulation of a new style for the twentieth century. The

FIGURE 67 Frank Lloyd Wright, Barnsdall House, Los Angeles, constructed 1920. (H. T. Wijdeveld, ed., *The Life-Work of the American Architect Frank Lloyd Wright* [Santpoort, Holland, 1925], 135)

FIGURE 68 Irving Gill, part of Lewis Courts, Sierra Madre, California, 1910. (*The Architect and Engineer of California*, June 1919, 75)

FIGURE 69 Hoover House, north corner of garden side. (Author)

FIGURE 70 Hoover House, main terrace on garden side. (Courtesy Stanford University Archives)

Hoover House is unusual, in this context, mainly because its principal designer, Lou Henry Hoover, was an amateur and did not think of herself as part of an avant-garde movement. Essentially, she was simply building a home for her family. But she thought carefully about the kind of architecture she considered functional and beautiful and, in the process, drew on qualities she admired in "primitive houses in many lands."

REFERENCE MATTER

STANFORD PRESIDENTS WHO HAVE LIVED IN THE HOUSE

Donald B. Tresidder (president 1943–48) and Mary Curry Tresidder.
J. E. Wallace Sterling (president 1949–68) and Ann Sterling.
Kenneth S. Pitzer (president 1968–70) and Jean Mosher Pitzer.
Richard W. Lyman (president 1970–80) and Elizabeth "Jing" Lyman.
Donald Kennedy (president 1980–92) and Jeanne Kennedy; Robin Kennedy.
Gerhard Casper (president 1992–2000) and Dr. Regina Casper.
John L. Hennessy (president 2000–) and Andrea Hennessy.

NOTES

Abbreviations

HH	Herbert Hoover
HHPL	Herbert Hoover Presidential Library, West Branch, Iowa
HHse	Hoover House
HIA	Hoover Institution Archives, Stanford University
LHH	Lou Henry Hoover
SUA	Stanford University Archives

Introduction

1. Letter from Herbert Hoover (HH) to Parmer Fuller, chairman of Stanford's Board of Trustees, December 27, 1944, HHPL, LHH Papers. Hoover explained that the house had belonged to his wife and was bequeathed to their sons on her death; he was buying it from the sons and giving it to the university "for the President's residence." One condition of the gift was that "it should be known as the Lou Henry Hoover House." The Hoovers themselves often referred to the house by its address, 623 Mirada Avenue (information from Dwight Miller, HHPL, August 2001). According to Anne Beiser Allen (*An Independent Woman: The Life of Lou Henry Hoover* [Westport, CT, 2000], 171), both of the Hoovers "had decided to turn the Stanford house over to the university."

2. Birge Clark (in "Memoirs About Mr. and Mrs. Herbert Hoover, With Particular Emphasis on the Planning and Building of their Home on San Juan Hill" [Palo Alto, CA, 1969], 23) says the second garage was added "after 1935." A blueprint of "Garage Addition," in SUA, is dated 1935.

3. Letter from Lou Henry Hoover (LHH) to Anna Hong Rutt, October 30, 1933, 2, HHPL, LHH Papers. See Chapter 2 for more on the surface and color of the house.

4. This garden wall, with an arched doorway in it, is seen in early photographs, for example one published in Arthur B. Clark, *Art Principles in House, Furniture, and Village Building* (Stanford, CA, 1921), 47.

5. See Chapter 3 for sources of these quotations. Herbert's "Hopi house" remark was first brought to my attention by Stanford student Bill Shen in 1998.

6. Birge Clark stated that this quotation was "something my father prepared for an article (which Mrs. Hoover approved)" ("Memoirs," 21); the comment also appears in a letter from Birge Clark to Mrs. W. Carmon Roberts, editor of *Arts and Decoration* December 11, 1928, SUA, HHse Papers.

7. B. Clark, "Oral History Interview . . . By Raymond Henle, January 19, 1970," 3, HHPL.

8. Letter from LHH to Anna Hong Rutt, October 30, 1933, 1, HHPL, LHH Papers.

9. Letter from Arthur B. Clark to LHH, undated but clearly early in the design process, HHPL, LHH Papers. See Chapter 2 for more about this letter.

10. B. Clark, "Memoirs," 4.

Chapter 1

1. B. Clark, "Memoirs," 6.

2. Herbert Hoover, *Memoirs of Herbert Hoover*, 2 vols. (New York, 1952), 5.

3. George H. Nash, *Herbert Hoover and Stanford University* (Stanford, CA, 1988), 29–31, 65–67. In 1922 the central building of the complex was completed; the Hoovers again provided a large portion of the needed funds. For more on the Men's and Women's Clubhouses, see Chapter 4.

4. It has been claimed that LHH was the first woman in the United States to receive a degree in geology, but geologist Judith Smith, of the Stanford University Geology Department, has told me that several women preceded her (correspondence with Judith Smith, 2002).

5. Letter from B. Clark to Mrs. W. Carmon Roberts, of *Arts and Decoration* magazine, December 11, 1928, SUA, HHse Papers.

6. Allen, *Independent Woman*, 1.

7. Information largely from Allen, *Independent Woman*.

8. See *The National Geographic Magazine*, September 1932, 362.

9. LHH to Anna Hong Rutt, October 30, 1933, 1, HHPL, LHH Papers. Quoted more fully in Chapter 3.

10. Regarding the Hoovers' racial views: Donald J. Lisio, *Hoover, Blacks, and Lily-Whites* (North Carolina, 1985), esp. ch. 2, 21–33; Allen, *Independent Woman*, 75, 83, 130–32.

11. Item in list of notes attached to letter from LHH to Arthur B. Clark, undated but probably of 1919; included in documents appended to Clark's "Memoirs," in which it is mentioned on p. 10.

12. The designation is "Bedroom" on the blueprints dated September 1919 (SUA, HHse Papers). The floor plans Birge Clark included in his "Memoirs" are labeled "ground floor [etc.] plan of Hoover House using nomenclature of 1919 preliminary studies."

13. Lisio, *Hoover*, 33.

14. For these friends, see Allen, *Independent Woman*. Correspondence between them and LHH is in HHPL, LHH Papers.

15. Allen, *Independent Woman*, 137, 156.

16. Ibid., 8.

17. Will Irwin, *Herbert Hoover: A Reminiscent Biography* (New York, 1928), 64–65; cited in Susan E. Kennedy, "Lou Henry's California," text of talk at Hoover Symposium XII, October 23, 1999, 6.

18. Allen, *Independent Woman*, ch. 9.

19. "Mrs. Hoover, Too, Has Served the Nation," *The New York Times Magazine*, July 22, 1928, 3.

20. "Electing a President's Wife," *Woman's Home Companion*, April 1928, 11.

21. Allen, *Independent Woman*, 154, 164, 166, 171.

22. B. Clark, letters to Harold Carewe, September 12, 1928, and Lillian Ferguson, July 7, 1928, both in SUA, HHse Papers. In the letter of July 7, Clark also wrote, "Mrs. Hoover herself is largely responsible for the general type of design, as her original requirements were [*sic*] that the house have all the roofs available for living purposes."

23. Letter from LHH to Anna Hong Rutt, October 30, 1933, 3.

24. See Chapter 5.

25. Letter from LHH to "Mrs. Campbell," June 14, 1923, HHPL, LHH Papers.

26. B. Clark, "Memoirs," 11.

27. Allen, *Independent Woman*, 169.

28. Ibid., 136. As a teenager, Lou had lived with her family in the Quaker town of Whittier, California; although Episcopalian, they had often attended the local Quaker meeting house (Allen, *Independent Woman*, 10).

29. Nash, *Hoover and Stanford*, 23–24.

30. Allen, *Independent Woman*, 1–2.

31. Ibid., 121.

32. Letter from LHH to Anna Hong Rutt, January 12, 1934, 1, HHPL, LHH Papers. "House building and decoration interest me so exceedingly that I have often wished that I had time to make a profession of it."

33. A 1928 article on Lou ("Mrs. Hoover, Too, Has Served the Nation," *New York Times Magazine*, July 22, 1928, 3) said she was "fascinated by architecture and has planned at least three houses." These are identified as the house at Stanford; the demonstration house Lou acquired for the Girl Scouts in Washington; and a project described as follows: "During the Food Administration period, Mrs. Hoover personally planned and financed the new quarters built for the thousands of extra girl clerks then in Washington." I have not been able to find what this refers to.

34. Allen, *Independent Woman*, 93–94.

35. Joy Scott, "Mrs. Hoover's Cottages," *Historic Houses of Lower San Juan Hill* (Stanford Historical Society, 1988), 32–40. Allen, *Independent Woman*, 108, 159–60.

36. B. Clark, "Memoirs," 29.

37. William Seale, *The President's House, A History* (Washington DC, 1986), 887; brought to my attention by Hank Dunlop. Allen, *Independent Woman*, 122–24. Lou reportedly gave architectural advice to two White House staff members planning to

build their own house (Ruth Dennis, *The Homes of the Hoovers* [West Branch, IA, 1986], 44).

38. Darwin Lambert, *Herbert Hoover's Hideaway: The Story of Camp Hoover on the Rapidan River* (Luray, VA, 1971). Allen, *Independent Woman*, 124–25.

39. Letter from HH to Mrs. Arthur Brown ("My dear Jessamine"), August 1960; photocopy provided to me by Jeffrey Tilman. According to Professor Tilman, the original is in a collection of Arthur Brown papers given to Stanford University in 2002.

40. Allen, *Independent Woman*, 157.

Chapter 2

1. For the Red House, see F. H. W. Sheppard, ed. *Survey of London*, vol. 37 (London, 1973), 71–72; Dennis, *Homes of the Hoovers*, 28–31. Regarding the furnishings, see B. Clark, "Memoirs," 12.

2. Dennis, *Homes of the Hoovers*, 32, 59–60; and more complete lists of the Hoovers' residences in HHPL, "Hoover Homes" file. The periods of residence at Stanford and in Palo Alto started mainly in 1914. In some cases only Lou and the Hoover sons were in California. In 1912 the family had leased a house in San Francisco and had considered building a house in that city, according to Nash, *Hoover and Stanford*, 192, n. 50.

3. Helen B. Pryor, *Lou Henry Hoover: Gallant First Lady* (New York, 1969), 83. Pryor had been an acquaintance of Lou's and apparently based much of her information on conversations with her.

4. The address of the house was originally 1 Reservoir Drive (B. Clark, "Memoirs," 6), then 623 Mirada Avenue.

5. Herbert later recalled, regarding Lou's planning of the house, "She had leased the lot some years before" (*Memoirs of Herbert Hoover*, 2:5). I have not been able to find the date of the lease or the document itself.

6. Nash, *Hoover and Stanford*, 56; source given as telegrams of May 14–15, 1917.

7. Mullgardt, in a letter to LHH, March 30, 1917 (HHPL, LHH Papers), wrote: President Wilbur told me today that you contemplated erecting a residence . . . and suggested that I advise you of my return, as you had expressed a desire to engage my services for this work." A second letter, the following day, reported that Mullgardt had visited the property, with Mrs. Wilbur, and that he was enclosing "the customary agreement form between Architect and Owner."

8. B. Clark, "Memoirs," 4.

9. Robert Judson Clark, "The Life and Architectural Accomplishment of Louis Christian Mullgardt, 1866–1942," Master's thesis, Stanford University, 1964. The ornament originally on the DeYoung Museum was later removed.

10. *Architect and Engineer*, December 1917, 98–99.

11. "Recent Work of Mr. Louis C. Mullgardt," *Architect and Engineer*, October 1917, 91. Brought to my attention by Robert J. Clark.

12. *San Francisco Examiner*, October 13, 1917, 10. Brought to my attention by Robert J. Clark. That it was picked up by the national press was mentioned by B. Clark, "Memoirs," 4.

13. Draft of letter from LHH to "My Dear Judge Lindley," undated, written on stationery inscribed "1701 Massachusetts Avenue, Washington, D.C." (where the family was living in the latter part of 1917), HHPL, LHH Papers.

14. B. Clark, "Memoirs," 3. This was the house of Prof. Albert C. Whitaker, now numbered 746 Santa Ynez St. See also Nash, *Hoover and Stanford*, 56, and "Historic Houses of San Juan Hill" (Stanford Historical Society, 1995).

15. According to Nash, she "immediately approached" Clark following a cable from Herbert of January 6, 1919 (*Hoover and Stanford*, 57).

16. According to Clark's son Birge, "My parents knew Mr. and Mr. Hoover from their days as Stanford students" ("Memoirs," 2). Arthur Bridgman Clark (1866–1948) had an architecture degree from the University of Syracuse and joined the Stanford faculty as art teacher when the university opened in 1891. The department he headed was called by various names in its early years (Drawing, Graphic Arts, and so on), but Birge Clark identified his father as "head of the Art Department" ("Memoirs," 4).

17. B. Clark, "Memoirs," 2; "Statement of Birge Clark," August 23, 1968, 1.

18. "In 1909 my father built our home at what is now 767 Santa Ynez Street" (B. Clark, "Memoirs," 6). "The Hoovers were living 100 yards away" (B. Clark, "Memo," February 10, 1965, 1). The Clark house now has the address 618 Mirada Ave. See "Historic Houses of San Juan Hill."

19. Letter from A. B. Clark to LHH, September 27, 1917, HHPL, LHH Papers.

20. Letter from A. B. Clark to LHH, undated (but before Birge Clark joined the team in early 1919), HHPL, LHH Papers.

21. A. B. Clark, *Art Principles*, 47.

22. Various documents indicate different dates, from January to March, 1919, for Birge's return to Stanford; in his "Memoirs," 5, he recalls it as either February or March.

23. For these writings of Birge Clark, see the Bibliography. For Birge Clark's life in general: *Sandstone and Tile* (spring–summer 1986): 3–9. He lived from 1893 to 1989.

24. B. Clark, "Memo," 1; "Memoirs," 4; "Statement," 2.

25. B. Clark, "Memoirs," 4. Clark adds that Davis was also involved in the design of "the Blaney residence near Saratoga, which was more the early California style" (in contrast to the "somewhat Provincial Georgian" style of Filoli). Clark notes that Davis was hired on a "week to week basis," and "while he was not a university trained man, he was very well schooled by the apprentice system." In an earlier statement, Clark identified Davis as more than just a draftsman; he said his father had "engaged Davis as temporary architect" (interview with Clark by Carol Green Wilson, June 30, 1950, HIA). A. B. Clark, *Art Principles*, 47, gives Davis's name as Charles T. Davis.

26. Undated letter to LHH from A. B. Clark, HHPL, LHH Papers.

27. B. Clark, "Memoirs," 5.

28. B. Clark, "Statement," 2. This information is found also in Clark's "Memoirs," 5, with the added detail that "once in a while I got to design and draw some less important interiors, including the fireplaces in the two sons' rooms."

29. B. Clark, "Memo," 1.

30. B. Clark, "Memoirs," 4.

31. B. Clark, "Memo," 2.

32. B. Clark, "Memoirs," 7.

33. Letter from Dare Stark to Laurine A. Small, February 1919, quoted in Allen, *Independent Woman*, 79, and cited as being in HHPL, LHH correspondence files.

34. Telegraph message in Kenneth Cosgrove papers, HHPL, according to Allen, *Independent Woman*, 79.

35. *Hoover, Memoirs of Herbert Hoover*, 2:5. Also relevant is the statement, quoted earlier, by Helen Pryor that as early as 1912 Lou "began sketching her ideas" for the house (*Lou Henry Hoover*, 83).

36. In his 1969 "Memoirs," for instance, Clark stated that Herbert "influenced the house by saying 'Make it structurally fireproof,' so it was built with a reinforced concrete skeleton" (15). Arthur B. Clark had also written, "When Mr. Hoover was asked for his wishes concerning the house his remark was characteristically brief and far-reaching; he said, 'Make it fire proof.'" ("House of Herbert Clark Hoover," 3, probably written in the 1920s).

37. B. Clark, "Statement," 2.

38. Pryor, *Lou Henry Hoover*, 119. "Lou Hoover, herself, designed the fireplace on one terrace and insisted that the three levels of terraces all be furnished for out-of-door living with a tennis court on one and a swimming pool on another for the boys." This is somewhat ambiguous, as it is unclear whether the ground level is being considered one of the terraces. Pryor's book was evidently based on conversations with Lou; they were acquaintances.

39. "Electing a President's Wife: Mrs. Hoover in the White House," *Woman's Home Companion*, April 1928, 11.

40. B. Clark, "Statement," 2; "Oral History Interview" (1970), 3. In the first case, the sentence continues, "and after various preliminary sketches of tile roofed residences, ruled tile out as seeming too pretentious and manorlike."

41. "Hoover's homely phrase was the best guide: 'It should look as if a child had piled up blocks,'" interview of Clark by Carol Green Wilson, 1950, HIA. In a letter of 1928, to be quoted in Chapter 3, Clark implied that Lou also wanted the house to look "like blocks piled up." However, since Clark made so few remarks about Herbert's input to the design, his statement that Herbert had this idea seems convincing.

42. Frank Lloyd Wright, *An Autobiography* (1932; reprint, New York, 1977), 33–34.

43. Telegram, January 6, 1919, quoted in Nash, *Hoover and Stanford*, 57.

44. B. Clark, "Memoirs," 4–5.

45. Several of these sheets of paper with sketches are in SUA, HHse Papers. They are not signed by LHH, but photocopies of a couple of them were appended by Birge Clark to his "Memoirs" and referred to, in his text, as being by LHH. The similarity of the drawing style on all the sheets, as well as the presence of LHH's handwriting on most of them, indicates that they were all drawn by her.

46. B. Clark, "Memoirs," 5.

47. Letter from LHH to A. B. Clark, undated, SUA, HHse Papers; photocopy appended to copy of B. Clark's "Memoirs."

48. These "suggestions" are apparently a three-page list of questions and thoughts, photocopy of which accompanies a photocopy of Lou's letter appended to B. Clark's "Memoirs," SUA, HHse Papers.

49. This sketch is one of the photocopied items included with B. Clark's "Memoirs." The original drawing is in SUA, HHse Papers.

50. Birge Clark later wrote, "In the early studies the terrace of the living room was broader and curved out, while the lower rooms followed the curve. This was ruled out by Mrs. Hoover as being a little too much in the grand manner" ("Memoirs," 7). Lou's letter shows that her objections to the curving façade were more substantive than Birge implied.

51. B. Clark, "Memoirs," 6.

52. Letter from LHH to Anna Hong Rutt, October 30, 1933, 1–2, HHPL, LHH Papers.

53. Ibid., 2; see also LHH to B. Clark, July 2, 1928, and B. Clark, "Memoirs," 9.

54. Letter from A. B. Clark to LHH, undated but early in the design, before Birge Clark joined the project, HHPL, LHH Papers, Hoover Homes collection.

55. B. Clark, "Memoirs," 7.

56. SUA, HHse Papers.

57. B. Clark, "Memoirs," 7. A similar "water spout" is on the south side of the house.

58. Letter from Allan Hoover to HH, June 17, 1919, HHPL. Birge Clark later recalled that "we started the house before the drawings were finished" ("Memoirs," 1).

59. There are a number of letters between Lou and Birge regarding the shipping of these items and damage that occurred to some of the furniture (for example, letters of March 15, 1920, July 13, 1920, February 22, 1921, and July 11, 1921), SUA, HHse Papers. As for the fireplace, a letter from LHH to Birge Clark, of July 2, 1928, indicates that Lou was considering installing it in the basement of the house ("it is the one to which Mr. Hoover attaches special sentiment").

60. Letter from LHH to Anna Hong Rutt, October 30, 1933, 2, HHPL, LHH papers. See also Allen, *Independent Woman*, 80, 82; Dennis, *Homes of the Hoovers*, 28.

61. LHH (from 19 Rue Lubeck, Paris) to B. Clark, August 4, 1919, SUA, HHse Papers.

62. B. Clark, "Memoirs," 9.

63. Ibid., 2.

64. Letter from LHH to Victor Horta, November 8, 1919, appended to copy of B. Clark's "Memoirs," SUA, HHse Papers.

65. Letters from LHH to Horta, December 13, 1919, and April 30, 1920, HHPL, LHH Papers.

66. B. Clark, "Memoirs," 20.

67. SUA, HHse Papers.

68. B. Clark, "Memoirs," 21–22.

69. Letter from LHH (on Shoreham Hotel, Washington, stationery), February 14, 1920, to "Mr. Clarke." Photocopy in documents appended to B. Clark's "Memoirs."

70. Noting only the locations specified in the surviving correspondence of early 1920, Lou was first at Stanford, then Washington DC (at the Shoreham Hotel), New York (933 Park Avenue), Washington (1228 17th Street), New York (55 East 77th Street), Stanford, New York (876 Park Avenue), and Stanford again. Correspondence between LHH and B. Clark, December 1919 to July 1920, SUA and HHPL.

71. Regarding the surface of the terraces: letters and telegrams between LHH and B. Clark, February 20, March 3 (multiple correspondence), June 9, and June 11, 1920, HHPL, LHH Papers; Clark, "Memoirs," 11, 14, 18. One of the letters of March 3 reveals that Lou had wanted the cement to be greenish in color, but Clark discovered that this was difficult to accomplish.

72. B. Clark, "Memoirs," 11.

73. Letter from LHH to Victor Horta, December 13, 1919, cited above.

74. Letter from LHH to Anna Hong Rutt, October 30 1933, 2.

75. LHH to Victor Horta, December 13, 1919; LHH to B. Clark, August 4, 1919, SUA. The letter to Horta speaks as if the colored surface already existed, but that was not yet the case.

76. Letter from B. Clark to LHH, June 15, 1920, HHPL, LHH Papers.

77. B. Clark, "Memoirs," 19.

78. Letter from LHH to Anna Hong Rutt, October 30, 1933, 2, HHPL, LHH Papers.

79. B. Clark, "Memoirs," 19. I have not been able to find the date of the first painting of the house. Bruce Wiggins and Kathleen Baldwin, of Stanford Facilities Operations, have told me that when the house has been repainted in recent times, the color has simply been matched to the existing paint.

80. Letter from LHH to B. Clark, July 29, 1921 (and accompanying sketch). Other letters of February 20 and March 3, 1920, and November 2, 1922. The swimming pool is mentioned in letters of March 4 and June 15, 1920.

81. SUA, HHse Papers.

82. *Sunset Magazine*, September 1928, 56; *San Francisco Chronicle*, July 1, 1928, Rotogravure Pictorial Section, 3.

83. B. Clark, "Memoirs," 8.

84. According to Birge Clark, "There wasn't a tremendous amount of yard left [for landscaping] on the downhill side of the house as the Cubberley yard came way up into the present yard" ("Memoirs," 8).

85. Letter from LHH to B. Clark, March 4, 1920, photocopy appended to B. Clark's "Memoirs."

86. Letter from LHH to B. Clark, March 15, 1920, as above.

87. Letter from A. B. Clark to LHH, June 19. 1920, HHPL, LHH Papers.

88. The first three figures are noted in Susan E. Kennedy's "Lou Henry Hoover's California," 12 and nn. 81–83; B. Clark, "Memoirs," 10.

89. B. Clark, "Memoirs," 4.

90. LHH to Anna Hong Rutt, October 30, 1933, 4.

91. Unidentified typescript, "Hoover to Have Month's Play with His Boys," HIA. This may be the "press release" of September 27, 1919 cited by Susan E. Kennedy as being from the "Public Statements file" ("Lou Henry Hoover's California," 12 and n. 79).

92. Allen, *Independent Woman*, 83.

93. These were Dare Stark and Philippi Harding (ibid., 83).

94. B. Clark, "Memoirs," 25.

95. "Hoover Home Is Closely Guarded," *The Bakersfield Californian*, June 1, 1929, 13. Brought to my attention by John Edward Powell.

96. Kennedy, "Lou Henry Hoover's California," 14.

97. Ibid., 16.

98. LHH to Anna Hong Rutt, October 30, 1933, HHPL, LHH Papers.

Chapter 3

1. Dare Stark (personal secretary of LHH), letter to Laurine A. Small, February 1919 (cited in Allen, *Independent Woman*, 78). "[The house] is going to be unique—pueblo Mexican Spanish with flat roofs."

2. A. B. Clark, *Art Principles*, 47. "Prototypes for its style [from] Mediterranean countries [and] country houses in Italy and Southwest United States."

3. *Cleveland Plain Dealer*, June 1928 (newspaper clipping in SUA HHse Papers). "The architecture is what is known as the Zuni Pueblo style."

4. "Hoover's Home at Stanford," *San Francisco Chronicle*, July 1, 1928. "[The house] is in the so-called Mission-Pueblo style of architecture."

5. Mary Fanton Roberts, "California Home of Mr. and Mrs. Herbert Hoover," *Arts and Decoration*, February 1929, 44–47, 118. "The exterior of the house is a prophecy of modernistic building today."

6. "Front façade . . . showing the Oriental square form and Moorish arched doorway" (ibid., 44); "the succession of terraces which suggest the Oriental inspiration" (ibid., 46).

7. Letter from Lillian Ferguson to B. Clark, July 6, 1929, SUA, HHse Papers.

8. Amanda M. Miller, "Republican Candidate's Home," *San Jose Mercury Herald*, August 12, 1928, clipping in HHPL, Hoover Homes Collection. "The Hispano-Moorish architecture of the structure."

9. *Sunset Magazine*, September 1928, 56. "Suggests the pueblo . . . but [is actually] Algerian."

10. *Architectural Progress*, February 1929, 8. "Hopi Indian [and] Algerian."

11. B. Clark, "Memoirs," 14–15. "The Hoovers did not want the house to be related to any historical style."

12. David Gebhard et al., *Guide to Architecture in San Francisco and Northern California* (Santa Barbara, 1973), 154. "[The house is a] large Mission Revival villa."

13. John Poppeliers et al., *What Style Is It?* (Washington DC, 1977), 40–41. "Qualities such as the cubistic forms and strong horizontal emphasis link it to the International Style." There are no doubt earlier characterizations of the house as International Style.

14. Lillian Ferguson to B. Clark, July , 1928. SUA, HHse Papers. Clark's reply is dated July 7, 1928.

15. Amanda M. Miller, "Republican Candidate's Home," *San Jose Mercury Herald*, August 12, 1928.

16. "California Home of Mr. and Mrs. Herbert Hoover," *Arts and Decoration*, February 1929, captions under photographs on 44, 46.

17. For example, the house is called "a large Mission Revival villa" in Gebhard et al., *Guide to Architecture*, 154.

18. The plaque, designating the house a California registered historical landmark, refers to "This 1919 residence of a developing International Style of architecture." Other designations of the house as International Style are found in: John Poppeliers et al., *What Style Is It?*; "International Style: Lou Henry Hoover House" (in an article on Stanford architecture), *Sandstone and Tile* (winter–spring 1987): 15–16; National Register nominations of the house, written by Dorothy Regnery, 1977, and James P. Delgado, 1984 ("unique in its design as an early example of the International Style"), SUA, HHse Papers.

19. Henry-Russell Hitchcock and Philip Johnson, *The International Style: Architecture Since 1922* (New York, 1932).

20. For Gill, see Thomas S. Hines, *Irving Gill and the Architecture of Reform* (New York, 2000); Bruce Kamerling, *Irving J. Gill, Architect* (San Diego, 1993).

21. In two historic-registration applications for the Hoover House of 1977, Dorothy Regnery provided information that could only have come from an interview with Birge Clark: "Although the final house was similar to a style to be popularized in Southern California at approximately the same time, Mrs. Hoover and the three architects were unaware of their contemporaries' designs" (National Register Nomination, June 1977, 1); "It is purely coincidental that the work of a contemporary architect in Southern California was somewhat similar" (Application for Historical Landmark status, July 1977, 2). Both documents are in SUA, HHse Papers.

22. Bertha H. Smith, "California's First Cubist House," *Sunset Magazine*, August 1915, 368–76; Irving Gill, "The Home of the Future: The New Architecture of the West," *The Craftsman*, May 1916, 140–51, 220. Also see, Eloise Roorbach, "Outdoor Life in California Houses, as Expressed in the New Architecture of Irving J. Gill," *The Craftsman*, July 1913, 435–38.

23. "The Home of the Future," 141–42, 147.

24. A. B. Clark, *Art Principles*, 47. "Southwestern United States" in this context must refer to Spanish types of country house, not to Pueblo Indian architecture, nor to the work of Irving Gill. In a later account, Clark repeated that the house had "prototypes in the Mediterranean countries" (undated notes by A. B. Clark, "The House of Herbert Hoover," 3; transcription in HIA). In "Memoirs," 7, Birge Clark said that his father designed "outside stairs" of the Hoover House "reminiscent of some he had seen in Italy."

25. B. Clark to Lillian Ferguson, July 7, 1928, SUA, HHse Papers.

26. The article that appeared in *Sunset Magazine* ("The California Home of Mr. and Mrs. Herbert Clark Hoover," September 1928, 56) stated that the house "suggests the pueblo influence [but is actually] Algerian."

27. Letter from Dare Stark to Laurine A. Small, February 1919; quoted in Allen, 79 and cited as being in HHPL, LHH correspondence files.

28. *Cleveland Plain Dealer*, June 18, 1928; clipping included in addendum to B. Clark's "Memoirs." An article in the *San Francisco Chronicle* ("Hoover's Home at Stanford," July 1, 1928, Rotogravure Pictorial Section, 3) identified the style as "Mission-Pueblo."

29. "Präsident Hoovers Sommerhaus in Kalifornien," *Die Dame*, Erstes Maiheft, 1929, 7–8, 52 (". . . Vorbildern, die sie [Mrs. Hoover] in Algier gesehen hat").

30. B. Clark to Harold Carewe, September 12, 1928, SUA, HHse Papers; the letter reveals that Carewe was a journalist or magazine editor, but the periodical is not specified. In the same archival source are other, similar letters written by Clark to journalists and magazine editors. A letter of December 11, 1928 to Mrs. W. Carmon Roberts, of the magazine *Arts and Decoration*, includes verbatim the passage quoted above from the letter to Carewe.

31. Perry F. Hoisington, editor of *Architectural Progress*, to B. Clark, December 7, 1928, SUA, HHse Papers.

32. B. Clark to Perry F. Hoisington, December 12, 1928. Source as above. Despite Clark's remarks, the article that subsequently appeared in *Architectural Progress* ("Residence of President-Elect Herbert C. Hoover," February 1929, 8) spoke of "Hopi Indian" as well as "Algerian" sources.

33. B. Clark, "Memoirs," 14, 15. As late as 1950, however, Birge was speaking of Algerian architecture as an influence, not just a coincidental similarity; in an interview of that year he said, "From the white-plastered houses of Algiers they [Lou and Herbert] drew inspiration for the exterior" (interview by Carol Green Wilson, January 30, 1950; transcription in HIA). The view that the house had no historical influence is found also in a text said to have been written by Arthur B. Clark in the 1920s; it states, "The house developed directly in response to its own individual circumstances without thought for conventional symmetry or provincial precedent" ("The House of Herbert Hoover, Secretary of Commerce, at Stanford University, California," 4–page typescript, copy in HIA; 1). This document is undated and anonymous, but a note appended by Birge Clark in 1965 identifies his father as the author and says it was written "when Mr. Hoover was first made Sec. of Commerce [1921], or . . . in 1928 when [he] became a potential candidate for the Presidency."

34. Birge Clark, quoted in "Lou Henry Hoover House Dedicated as California State Landmark," unidentified newspaper clipping in SUA, HHse Papers, probably from *Campus Report*, early 1978.

35. B. Clark, "Memoirs," 7.

36. Hoover, *Memoirs of Herbert Hoover*, 2:5.

37. Letter from LHH to "Sue" (Susan Dyer), July 13, 1928. HIA, Dyer Box 6. An epigraph at the front of this book gives this quotation more fully.

38. Correspondence between Anna Hong Rutt and LHH: letter from Rutt to LHH, October 14, 1933: reply from LHH, October 30, 1933; second letter from Rutt, November 28, 1933; reply from LHH, January 12, 1934. The letters from Rutt and copies of Lou's letters are in HHPL, LHH Papers. Lou's letters are in HIA. The photographs Lou enclosed with her first letter are not known to have survived. The book Rutt was writing was evidently *Home Furnishing*, published first in 1935. I have seen only the second edition of the work (New York, 1948), which has no reference to the Hoover House. In her second letter, Rutt said she would like to write a separate article on the house; in reply, Lou said she had no objection, but it is not known if the article ever appeared.

39. LHH to Anna Hong Rutt, October 30, 1933, 1.

40. "The term 'Moorish' carried rather vague connotations at that time [c. 1900, in California]. Many people had the impression that the missions contained elements of Moorish design. Often, too, the term was used to describe any elements in Spanish architecture that seemed exotic" (Richard Longstreth, *On the Edge of the World* [New York, 1983], 387, n. 15).

Chapter 4

1. HHPL, LHH Papers, subject files "School Papers" and "Articles."

2. The dates of these moves differ slightly in various sources. See Allen, *Independent Woman*, 7–10; Kennedy, "Lou Henry Hoover's California," 1–2; Colbert, *Lou Henry Hoover: The Duty to Serve*, 10–12; Dennis, *Homes of the Hoovers*, 20, 58.

3. HHPL, LHH Papers, subject file "School Papers." The essay "Indians," apparently a continuation of the "Mound Builders" essay, is dated "February 1886, Room 10, Waterloo Public School." The "Acoma" essay is in the same subject file. "The Missions of California" is in "Articles, Addresses, etc., 1886–98."

4. For the Henrys' journey by the Atchison, Topeka and Santa Fe Railroad (changed to Railway in 1895), see Colbert, *Lou Henry Hoover*, 12; Kennedy, "Lou Henry Hoover's California," 2. Already in the 1880s this railroad was publicizing the Pueblo culture of the Southwest to its passengers. "Travelers, passing the Pueblo villages . . . in the eighties were invited to recall the villages of ancient Egypt [etc.]" (Ernest Pomeroy, *In Search of the Golden West . . .* [New York, 1957], 39, as quoted in Martha Weigle and Barbara A. Babcock, eds., *The Great Southwest of the Fred Harvey Company and the Santa Fe Railway* [Phoenix, 1996], 6).

5. Frank H. Cushing, "My Adventures in Zuñi," *The Century Illustrated Monthly Magazine*, December 1882, 191–207; February 1883, 500–11; May 1883, 28–47.

6. HHPL, LHH Papers, subject file "Diaries, 1889–92," diary entry of December 26, 1889. "The house is quite large, a story and a half high, built of adobe, whitewashed, and having a large wooden veranda in front, facing an orange orchard. On the western side is a veranda enclosed on both sides" (p. 5 of this entry).

7. Colbert, *Lou Henry Hoover*, 20.

8. HHPL, LHH Papers, subject file "School Papers, Sketches, 1889–95." It is likely that some of these sketches were drawn from published illustrations, not from life (for

example, the San Gabriel Mission drawing, with a trompe-l'oeil border typical of magazine and book illustration of the period).

9. Nash, *Life of Herbert Hoover*, 1:9, 584 n. 64; Hoover, *Memoirs of Herbert Hoover*, 1:4–5.

10. HHPL, LHH Papers, correspondence with Mary Austin, letter of June 14, 1923.

11. Nash, *Life of Herbert Hoover*, 1:47.

12. David Starr Jordan, *The Days of a Man* (New York, 1922), 1:620–37. Another photograph from this 1898 trip, showing Lummis photographing Indians, is credited to Jessie Knight Jordan in *Charles F. Lummis: Centennial Exhibition* (Los Angeles, 1985), 22; and Jane Apostol, *El Alisal: Where History Lingers* (Los Angeles, 1994), 36.

13. The letters and diaries are in HHPL, LHH Papers, the scrapbooks in HHPL, Hoover Scrapbooks collection.

14. HHPL, LHH Papers, subject file "Diaries, 1899," entry of c. April 1899 (most of LHH's diary entries are not precisely datable).

15. For their house in Tientsin, see Dennis, *Homes of the Hoovers*, 25–28.

16. For "pretentious," see diary entries c. January 1902, in Kalgoorlie, Australia, and c. January 1904, in Honolulu.

17. HHPL, Hoover Scrapbooks.

18. Among these trips to or across the United States, by Lou and/or Herbert (as indicated in a "Chronology" found in HHPL, LHH Papers, subject file "Trips, Travels, Residences"): trips of October 1901, July 1902, December 1903 to early 1904, January–June 1905, July–September 1906, December 1908 to May 1909, September 1909 to February 1911, July–August 1911.

19. Weigle and Babcock, *Great Southwest*.

20. HHPL, Scrapbooks, box 2, folder 18.

21. HHPL, LHH Papers, subject file "Indians." These are plates LXI, CX, and CXXV from *Twenty-third Annual Report of the Bureau of American Ethnology . . . 1901–1902* (Washington, 1904).

22. An article in *The National Geographic Magazine* of September 1932, about a National Geographic Society event attended by President and Mrs. Hoover, stated, "Mrs. Hoover has been a member of our Society for thirty years, joining it when it was a small group of some 2,500 members. Her encouragement and consistent support have greatly aided The Society" (362).

23. *The National Geographic Magazine*, February 1911, 107–37.

24. For Mary Austin, see Mary Austin, *Earth Horizon: Autobiography* (Boston, 1932); T. M. Pearce, ed., *Literary America 1903–1934: The Mary Austin Papers* (Westport, CT, 1979); Augusta Fink, *I-Mary, A Biography of Mary Austin* (Tucson, AZ, 1983). Correspondence between Austin and the Hoovers, see HHPL, HH and LHH Papers.

25. Correspondence between Mary Austin and LHH, 1919–22, in HHPL, LHH Papers, correspondence file Mary Austin, subject file "Indians," subject file "Paintings and Artwork Purchased by LHH, 1922–24." Also see Henry E. Huntington Library, San Marino, CA, Mary Austin Papers.

26. Letter from LHH to Mary Austin, undated; reproduced in Pearce, *Literary America 1903–1934*, 98. The editor suggests that the letter dates from March or April 1919, but it is surely earlier, as Lou would not have been speaking so speculatively about having "an Indian room some day" in the final stages of designing her house.

27. *San Jose Mercury News*, November 7, 1928; SUA, HHse Papers, information from Richard Joncas. According to Dwight M. Miller, HHPL, "Mrs. Hoover had a pronounced interest in Indians artists and Navajo rugs" (correspondence, November 3, 1998).

28. For the Rapidan Camp, see Darwin Lambert, *Herbert Hoover's Hideaway* (Luray, VA, 1971). Indian objects shown in photographs on pp. 31, 44, 50, 123, 125.

29. Letter and telegram from LHH to B. Clark, November 2, 1922, reproduced in B. Clark, "Memoirs."

30. Correspondence with Mary A. Van Stone and artist Olive Rush, November–December 1922, HHPL, LHH Papers, subject file "Paintings and Art Work Purchased by LHH, 1922–24." According to members of the Hoover family with whom I have communicated, it is not known what happened to these paintings, nor to the Indian pottery and rugs collected by Lou.

31. Mary A. Van Stone to LHH, November 25, 1922. The Jemez painting was by Vierra; it is not clear from the correspondence whether the Hoovers purchased it.

32. Letter from LHH to Jessie Jones, September 1, 1941, 4. HHPL, LHH Papers, Personal Correspondence file.

33. For the Pueblo Revival, see Nicholas C. Markovich, ed., *Pueblo Style and Regional Architecture* (New York, 1990).

34. This was the Bailey House, described and illustrated in "New Hopi Architecture," *The Craftsman*, July 1916, 374–82.

35. For the Fisher and Ward houses, see *The Architect and Engineer*, March 1911, 58; May 1912, 84. I am grateful to Lynn Horiuchi for showing me her research on Whittlesey.

36. Mrs. Harold M. Bacon, longtime Stanford resident, recalled in 1967, "I have heard tell that Herbert Hoover had been down in the Southwest and had been much impressed with the Mission Style architecture that the Harvey Co. was then using for its Harvey Houses along the Santa Fe railway line. Mr. Whittlesey had designed those buildings I am told, and so if you'll look closely you'll see four little towers or turrets on our building. This was to give the clubhouse an impression of a miniature Harvey House at Albuquerque." SUA, SC-491; brought to my attention by Ashish Vora, 1999.

37. G. H. Edgell, *The American Architecture of To-day* (New York, 1928), 66.

Chapter 5

1. LHH to Anna Hong Rutt, October 30, 1933, 1.

2. *The Craftsman*, July 1913, 434.

3. George Wharton James, *What the White Race May Learn from the Indian* (Chicago, 1908).

4. From an interview with Jean Pitzer by Germaine LaBerge, 1998, transcribed on the website of the Regional Oral History Office, Bancroft Library, Berkeley. Quoted with permission of the Regional Oral History Office.

5. LHH to Anna Hong Rutt, October 30, 1933, 3, 4.

6. Vere O. Wallingford, "A Type of Original American Architecture," *The Architectural Record*, June 1906, 469.

7. Judith Sheine, *R. M. Schindler* (London, 2001), 27–28. David Gebhard, *Schindler* (New York, 1971), 27–30.

8. For Wright's attraction to Mesoamerican and Native American architecture, see Anthony Alofsin, *Frank Lloyd Wright: The Lost Years, 1910–1922* (Chicago, 1993), ch. 8; Neil Levine, *The Architecture of Frank Lloyd Wright* (Princeton, NJ, 1996), 138–41, 172–73, 185–89.

9. Thomas S. Hines, *Irving Gill and the Architecture of Reform* (New York, 2000), 36, 70, 89, 211–12.

10. In 1911 Charles-Edouard Jeanneret (Le Corbusier) traveled in Eastern Europe, Turkey, and Greece and was struck by the vernacular architecture of these regions. He wrote of the experience in letters and articles, which he later published as a book: *Voyage d'Orient* (Paris, 1966). In the 1920s and 1930s Le Corbusier became interested also in the indigenous architecture of North Africa.

BIBLIOGRAPHY

Archival Sources

COLLECTIONS

Herbert Hoover Presidential Library (HHPL), West Branch, Iowa. Herbert Hoover Papers; Lou Henry Hoover Papers; Scrapbooks; Photograph Collection.

Hoover Institution Archives (HIA), Stanford University. Lou Henry Hoover Collection.

Stanford University Archives (SUA), Stanford University Library. Hoover House Papers; Lou Henry Hoover Papers; Birge Clark Papers; General Photograph Collection; Map Collection.

MANUSCRIPTS

[Clark, Arthur B.] "The House of Herbert Clark Hoover, Secretary of Commerce, at Stanford University, California." Undated ms., HIA.

Clark, Birge M. "Application for Registration of Historical Landmark," for Lou Henry Hoover House. December 9, 1975. Copy in SUA, HHse Papers.

Clark, Birge M. "Memo on Planning and Construction of the Hoover Home on the Stanford Campus." February 10, 1965. HIA

Clark, Birge M. "Memoirs About Mr. and Mrs. Herbert Hoover, With Particular Emphasis on the Planning and Building of their Home on San Juan Hill." March 1969, Palo Alto, CA. Copies in SUA, HHse Papers.

Clark, Birge M. "Oral History Interview with Birge M. Clark, By Raymond Henle. January 19, 1970." HIA

Clark, Birge M. "Statement of Birge Clark, Describing Various Contacts with Mr. & Mrs. Hoover." August 23, 1968. HIA

Delgado, James P. "National Register of Historic Places Inventory, Nomination Form," for Lou Henry Hoover House. July 23, 1984. SUA, HHse Papers.

Kennedy, Susan E. "Lou Henry Hoover's California." Text of address, George Fox University, October 23, 1999.

Regnery, Dorothy, F. "Application for Registration of Historical Landmark," for Lou Henry Hoover House. July 15, 1977. SUA, HHse Papers.

Bibliography

Printed Works

Allen, Anne Beiser. *An Independent Woman: The Life of Lou Henry Hoover*. Westport, CT, 2000.

Alofsin, Anthony. *Frank Lloyd Wright: The Lost Years, 1910–1922*. Chicago, 1993.

Apostol, Jane. *El Alisal: Where History Lingers*. Los Angeles, 1994.

Austin, Mary. *Earth Horizon: Autobiography*. Boston, 1932.

"The California Home of Mr. and Mrs. Herbert Clark Hoover." *Sunset Magazine*, September 1928, 56.

Charles F. Lummis: Centennial Exhibition. Los Angeles, 1985.

Clark, Arthur Bridgman. *Art Principles in House, Furniture, and Village Building*. Stanford, CA, 1921.

Clark, Birge M. "The Stanfords wanted a house that was livable. . . . " *Stanford Historical Society Newsletter* (spring–summer 1978): 4–6.

Colbert, Nancy. *Lou Henry Hoover: The Duty to Serve*. Greensboro, NC, 1998.

Dennis, Ruth. *The Homes of the Hoovers*. West Branch, IA, 1986.

Edgell, G. H. *The American Architecture of To-day*. New York, 1928.

Fink, Augusta. *I-Mary, A Biography of Mary Austin*. Tucson, AZ, 1983.

Gebhard, David. *Schindler*. New York, 1971.

Gebhard, David, et al. *Guide to Architecture in San Francisco and Northern California*. Santa Barbara, 1973.

Hines, Thomas S. *Irving Gill and the Architecture of Reform*. New York, 2000.

"Historic Houses of San Juan Hill." Stanford Historical Society, 1995.

Hitchcock, Henry-Russell, and Philip Johnson. *The International Style: Architecture Since 1922*. New York, 1932.

"Homey House Is Hoover Dwelling." *Cleveland Plain Dealer*, June 18, 1928.

Hoover, Herbert C. *The Memoirs of Herbert Hoover*. 2 vols. New York, 1952.

Hoover, Herbert C., and Lou Henry, trans. and eds. Agricola, *De re metallica*. London, 1912.

"Hoover Plans $50,000 Home." *The San Francisco Examiner*, October 13, 1917.

"Hoover's Home." *San Jose Mercury Herald*, August 12, 1928.

"Hoover's Home at Stanford." *San Francisco Chronicle*, July 1, 1928.

Irwin, Will. *Herbert Hoover: A Reminiscent Biography*. New York, 1928.

James, George Wharton. *What the White Race May Learn from the Indian*. Chicago, 1908.

Jeanneret, Charles-Edouard. *Voyage d'Orient*. Paris, 1966.

Jordan, David Starr. *The Days of a Man*. New York, 1922.

Kamerling, Bruce. *Irving J. Gill, Architect*. San Diego, 1993.

Lambert, Darwin. *Herbert Hoover's Hideaway: The Story of Camp Hoover on the Rapidan River*. Luray, VA, 1971.

Levine, Neil. *The Architecture of Frank Lloyd Wright*. Princeton, NJ, 1996.

Lisio, Donald J. *Hoover, Blacks, and Lily-Whites*. North Carolina, 1985.

Longstreth, Richard. *On the Edge of the World*. New York, 1983.

"Lou Henry Hoover House." Stanford, CA, n.d. (c. 1990s), brochure.
Markovich, Nicholas C., ed. *Pueblo Style and Regional Architecture*. New York, 1990.
"Mrs. Hoover, Too, Has Served the Nation." *The New York Times Magazine*, July 22, 1928, 3, 23.
Nash, George H. *Herbert Hoover and Stanford University*. Stanford, CA, 1988.
Nash, George H. *The Life of Herbert Hoover*. New York, 1983.
Pearce, T. M., ed. *Literary America 1903–1934: The Mary Austin Papers*. Westport, CT, 1979.
Pomeroy, Ernest. *In Search of the Golden West. . . .* New York, 1957.
Poppeliers, John, et al. *What Style Is It?* Washington DC, 1977.
"Präsident Hoovers Sommerhaus in Kalifornien." *Die Dame*, Erstes Maiheft, 1929, 7–8, 52.
Pryor, Helen B. *Lou Henry Hoover: Gallant First Lady*. New York, 1969.
"Residence for Mr. and Mrs. Herbert C. Hoover." *The Architect and Engineer*, December 1917, 98–99.
"Residence of President-Elect Herbert C. Hoover." *Architectural Progress*, February 1929, 8–10, 25.
Roberts, Mary Fanton. "California Home of Mr. and Mrs. Herbert Hoover." *Arts and Decoration*, February 1929, 44–47, 118.
Scott, Joy. "Mrs. Hoover's Cottages." *Historic Houses of Lower San Juan Hill*. Stanford Historical Society, 1988.
Seale, William. *The President's House, A History*. Washington DC, 1986.
Sheine, Judith. *R. M. Schindler*. London, 2001.
Sheppard, F. H. W., ed. *Survey of London*. Vol. 37. London, 1973.
Weigle, Martha, and Barbara A. Babcock, eds. *The Great Southwest of the Fred Harvey Company and the Santa Fe Railway*. Phoenix, 1996.
Wright, Frank Lloyd. *An Autobiography*. 1932; reprint, New York, 1977.

INDEX